The Paleo Green Feast

Ancient-Inspired Recipes for the Modern Table

VESELA EKSTEDT

Vesla Ekstedt

Table of Contents

Vesla Ekstedt

Introduction

Welcome to *The Caveman's Green Table: Paleo and Plant-Based Lifestyle for Men's Health,* a nutritional roadmap that combines the primal wisdom of our ancestors with the environmental awareness of the modern world. In the following pages, you'll find guidance and strategies that utilize the strengths of both the Paleo and plant-based diets, helping men to optimize their health, vitality, and longevity.

The Paleo, or "caveman" diet, centers around the concept of consuming the same types of foods as our hunter-gatherer ancestors. It harkens back to a time before agriculture, when our meals were sourced from the wild—meats, fish, fruits, vegetables, nuts, and seeds. Proponents of this dietary approach argue that our bodies are genetically predisposed to thrive on such foods, citing potential health benefits like improved weight management, increased energy, and a lower risk of chronic disease.

The plant-based diet, on the other hand, is a diet high in vegetables, fruits, grains, nuts, and seeds, while eschewing animal-based products. This diet has been lauded for its potential to support heart health, maintain a healthy weight, and reduce the risk of chronic diseases such as diabetes and certain cancers. Moreover, it offers a more sustainable choice for the environment, as plant-based diets generally require fewer resources and generate fewer greenhouse gas emissions compared to diets high in animal products.

The Caveman's Green Table strives to strike a balance between these two dietary perspectives, retaining the nutrient-dense, whole food focus of the Paleo diet while incorporating the healthful plant-centric aspects of a plant-based lifestyle. This innovative approach, we argue, provides a robust dietary framework that supports men's health in a unique and holistic way.

Chapter One sets the stage by tracing back our dietary history and giving you a closer look at the eating habits of our early ancestors, known as the cavemen, or the Paleolithic humans. As you journey into the pre-agricultural past, you'll begin to see how these early diets have influenced our eating habits and health today.

In the chapters that follow, you'll discover the core principles of both the Paleo and plant-based diets, learning about their potential benefits and drawbacks. Importantly, we aim to dispel some common misconceptions, such as the myth that Paleo diets must be high in meat and low in plant foods or that plant-based diets inherently lack sufficient protein.

The middle section of this book delivers practical guidance on how to successfully blend these two dietary approaches in real life. From understanding the balance of macronutrients to ensuring you're getting enough essential vitamins and minerals—we'll provide you with the knowledge you need to navigate your way to better health. You'll also find a collection of delicious and nourishing recipes to kick-start your journey toward a healthier, more balanced diet.

As we move towards the latter part of the book, we'll delve into scientific research around diet, longevity, and disease prevention. We'll also discuss the benefits of this combined diet for physical performance, and present exercise regimes that complement it.

The *Caveman's Green Table* aims to equip men with the tools they need to protect their hearts through diet. Additionally, men generally have higher daily caloric and protein requirements, which this dietary approach is designed to accommodate.

It's also essential to discuss the impact of diet on mental health. Depression, anxiety, and other mental health disorders are often overlooked in men, yet they are just as prevalent in this demographic as in women. Emerging research suggests that diet plays a critical role in mental health, with both the Paleo and plant-based diets showing promise in this regard. We'll delve into the science behind this and provide strategies for supporting mental well-being through diet.

The Paleo Green Feast

Moreover, one cannot discuss men's health without addressing the current obesity epidemic. According to the World Health Organization, globally, more men are obese than women. *The Caveman's Green Table* approach helps tackle this problem head-on by promoting nutrient-dense, satiating foods that aid in weight management.

To ensure your success, we've dedicated an entire chapter to meal prep mastery, recognizing that busy lifestyles can often be a barrier to healthy eating. In this section, we'll share tips and tricks for preparing healthy, delicious meals efficiently, making it easier to stick to your new dietary regimen even with a hectic schedule. You'll find a variety of quick and easy recipes that align with *The Caveman's Green Table* principles.

Lastly, it's essential to remember that, although the focus of this book is on dietary habits, a healthy lifestyle doesn't stop at what you eat. Exercise, stress management, and sufficient sleep are all critical components of overall health. In the later chapters, we'll provide comprehensive guidance on incorporating these elements to support your dietary changes and maximize health benefits.

So, whether you are looking to improve your physical performance, support your mental health, or simply learn more about how the right foods can improve your overall well-being, this book will serve as a valuable guide. We invite you to discover the transformative power of *The Caveman's Green Table* and look forward to supporting you on your journey towards enhanced health and vitality.

Your journey towards a healthier lifestyle starts here! Welcome to *The Caveman's Green Table!*

Vesla Ekstedt

Chapter 1

The Genesis of Diet - A Historical Perspective on Cavemen and Green Table

In this first chapter, we'll embark on a fascinating journey back in time to trace the genesis of the human diet and explore how our early ancestors, the cavemen, fed themselves in the pre-agricultural era. We'll study the principles and benefits of what is now known as the "Paleo diet" and its relevance in our current dietary landscape. Subsequently, we'll turn our attention to the modern concept of the Green Table, introducing you to the plant-based diet's fundamentals and benefits. By unearthing our dietary roots and linking this with modern nutritional wisdom, we aim to provide a robust understanding of these two dietary practices and how they intertwine.

I Understanding Paleo

The term "Paleo" is derived from the Paleolithic era, a period in human history that spanned from approximately 2.5 million to 10,000 years ago. During this time, humans lived as hunter-gatherers—their survival hinged on the food they could hunt or forage. This period predated the advent of agriculture, a critical point as it means the diet of our Paleolithic ancestors was devoid of grains, legumes, and dairy—food groups that would become staples only after the advent of farming.

The Paleo diet, often referred to as the caveman diet, is based on the principle of emulating the eating habits of our Paleolithic ancestors. It operates on the theory that our bodies are genetically adapted to thrive on the foods that were available to us before the Agricultural Revolution.

The Paleo diet is rich in lean meats, fish, fruits, vegetables, nuts, and seeds—foods that could be obtained by hunting and gathering. Conversely, it excludes food types that became common when farming emerged, like dairy products, legumes, and grains. Additionally, anything that appears to be a product of modern food processing, such as refined sugars, artificial sweeteners, and processed oils, also falls outside the realm of a Paleo diet.

One of the primary benefits of the Paleo diet is its focus on whole, unprocessed foods. In an era where processed and fast foods have become ubiquitous, returning to a diet based on whole foods can be a powerful strategy for health improvement.

Whole foods, as advocated by the Paleo diet, are rich in a variety of essential nutrients including fiber, healthy fats, quality protein, vitamins, and minerals. Consuming a diet high in these nutrient-dense foods can support optimal body function and prevent various health issues such as obesity, diabetes, heart disease, and certain cancers.

Moreover, the Paleo diet may contribute to improved gut health. Modern diets high in processed foods and refined sugars can disrupt the gut microbiota, leading to digestive issues and inflammatory responses. By eliminating these disruptive foods, the Paleo diet helps maintain a balanced and diverse gut microbiota.

However, it's also important to note the criticisms of the Paleo diet. Some nutritionists argue that the exclusion of whole grains and legumes, both of which are rich in fiber and other beneficial compounds, may not be in our best interest. Similarly, the omission of dairy can lead to insufficient calcium intake, potentially impacting bone health.

It's also worth noting that our Paleolithic ancestors' diet was likely extremely varied, depending on their specific geographic location and the season. Therefore, the modern interpretation of the Paleo diet may not be entirely accurate or comprehensive.

The key takeaway from understanding the Paleo diet is not to blindly mimic the dietary patterns of our ancestors, but to adapt the principles that can fit into our modern lifestyle and contribute to better health. In the following sections, we'll continue to explore these concepts, shedding more light on the Paleo lifestyle and its integration with the Green Table concept.

The Paleo Green Feast

II The Hunter-Gatherer Lifestyle

In this section, we take a deep dive into the world of our hunter-gatherer ancestors. To fully appreciate the Paleo diet, we need to understand the daily routines and survival mechanisms of these early humans.

Our Paleolithic ancestors were nomadic tribes that moved with the seasons and the migration patterns of the animals they hunted. Their survival depended on their knowledge of the environment, understanding animal behavior, and the ability to recognize edible plants.

Paleolithic humans were not simply carnivores. They consumed a mix of wild animals, fish, fruits, vegetables, nuts, and seeds. Unlike our modern diet, their food was free from artificial additives, preservatives, and was naturally low in sodium and high in fiber.

Their food procurement methods required considerable physical activity. Hunting required strategy, speed, and strength; while gathering plant-based food necessitated endurance and a detailed knowledge of edible plants and herbs. This active lifestyle, combined with a natural, nutrient-dense diet, allowed them to maintain excellent health, strength, and endurance.

Despite the appeal of their varied and natural diet, the hunter-gatherer lifestyle was not without its challenges. Food sources were not always reliable or abundant, leading to periods of scarcity or forced fasting. Nonetheless, these challenges also brought about resilience and adaptability, traits that allowed them to survive and thrive in various environments.

By understanding the hunter-gatherer lifestyle, we learn that our bodies evolved to be active and to consume a varied diet of whole, unprocessed foods.

III Food Sources and Nutrition

This section delves into the heart of the Paleolithic diet—the foods our ancestors ate and their nutritional profiles. Understanding the variety and nutrient content of these foods can further elucidate why the Paleo diet can be beneficial for modern men's health.

1. Meat and Fish: Paleolithic humans consumed a variety of wild game and fish. These sources of protein are rich in essential amino acids, which are crucial for muscle growth and repair, hormone regulation, and various body functions. Wild game is typically leaner than farmed meat and has a higher concentration of omega-3 fatty acids, which are beneficial for heart health. Fish, particularly fatty varieties like salmon and mackerel, are also rich in omega-3s and vitamin D.

2. Fruits and Vegetables: These were a significant component of the Paleolithic diet. Fruits and vegetables provide an array of essential vitamins, minerals, and fiber. They are also high in antioxidants and phytochemicals, compounds that help protect against chronic diseases like heart disease and cancer.

3. Nuts and Seeds: These were a valuable source of healthy fats, protein, fiber, and various micronutrients. They were likely consumed in moderation due to their high caloric content.

4. Roots and Tubers: Depending on the region and season, early humans would have consumed various roots and tubers, providing a source of complex carbohydrates, vitamins, and minerals.

While the foods that Paleolithic humans ate were nutritionally rich, it's important to note that they were consumed as part of a balanced, diverse diet and an active lifestyle. While our modern diets and lifestyles are quite different, understanding the nutrient profile and benefits of these foods can guide our own dietary choices.

IV From Paleolithic to Neolithic: The Dawn of Agriculture

One of the most profound shifts in human history was the transition from the Paleolithic era to the Neolithic era, often referred to as the Agricultural Revolution. This transition marked a significant change in human lifestyle and, consequently, our diets.

The Paleo Green Feast

The Agricultural Revolution began around 10,000 BC in the Fertile Crescent, a region in the Middle East known for its rich, arable land. Instead of a nomadic existence, humans began to settle in one place, cultivating crops and domesticating animals for food. This shift offered a more reliable and abundant food source, allowing populations to expand and civilizations to develop.

However, these changes also had a profound effect on the human diet. Instead of a varied diet of wild animals, fish, fruits, vegetables, and foraged plant foods, the diet began to rely heavily on a limited number of cultivated crops, primarily grains like wheat, barley, and later, corn and rice. Legumes, dairy products, and domesticated animal meats also became more prevalent.

While this shift allowed for more predictable food sources and the development of cooking and food preservation techniques, it also led to a decrease in dietary diversity and nutrient density. For example, while grains provide necessary carbohydrates and some vitamins and minerals, they lack the range of nutrients found in the wild foods of our hunter-gatherer ancestors.

The move to agriculture also led to other changes. Humans began consuming more carbohydrates and less protein, and their fat consumption shifted from primarily omega-3 fatty acids to a balance of omega-3 and omega-6 fatty acids. This change in dietary fat composition is believed to have health implications, with a higher omega-6 to omega-3 ratio associated with inflammation and increased risk of chronic diseases.

This transition is also when humans started consuming significant amounts of dairy. While dairy products provide valuable nutrients like protein, calcium, and vitamin D, they were absent in the Paleolithic diet, and some people may find them hard to digest, leading to intolerance or allergic reactions.

Finally, the shift to a sedentary agricultural lifestyle meant less physical activity, which, combined with a change in diet, set the stage for many modern health issues.

It is important to note that, while the Paleo diet is based on the premise that our bodies are better adapted to pre-agricultural foods, it doesn't mean we should entirely abandon foods that came with agriculture. Rather, the lesson is in the balance and variety of our diet, and in understanding how certain food types can affect our health.

As we reach the end of this foundational chapter, we can appreciate how our understanding of the past, particularly our ancestral dietary practices, can shape our present and future nutritional choices. We've seen how the Paleo diet, derived from our hunter-gatherer ancestors' lifestyle, champions the consumption of whole, unprocessed foods—a practice that is as beneficial today as it was in the Paleolithic era. Similarly, we've discussed the Agricultural Revolution's effects, which, while it introduced new dietary components, also decreased dietary diversity and influenced our health in complex ways.

This exploration serves as a reminder that our bodies are the products of millions of years of evolution, finely tuned to thrive on a varied, nutrient-dense diet, and an active lifestyle. As we turn to the next part of this book, where we explore the principles of the Green Table, we'll see how we can learn from both the Paleolithic and Neolithic periods, adopting the beneficial aspects of each, and discarding the detrimental ones.

Finally, we should bear in mind that the essence of this book is not to provide strict dietary rules, but rather guidelines and principles that can be adapted to our individual needs and circumstances. Our aim is to help you cultivate an understanding and appreciation for the food you eat, its origins, its nutritional content, and its impact on your health. By doing so, you'll be well-equipped to make informed dietary choices that align with both your health goals and the sustainability of our planet. Armed with this knowledge, we invite you to journey further with us into the world of *The Caveman's Green Table.*

Chapter 2
The Paleo Blueprint—Understanding the Caveman's Diet and Lifestyle

Journey with us as we delve into the fascinating world of our Paleolithic ancestors, exploring the principles that governed their diets and lifestyles. This chapter is not merely an exploration of what early humans ate, but a detailed inspection of a way of life that, although belonging to an era far removed from ours, has relevance and bearing on our contemporary health challenges. The Paleo diet, also known as the Caveman's diet, is more than simply a dietary regimen; it's a comprehensive lifestyle, encompassing a broad spectrum of activities and choices that extend far beyond the confines of the kitchen.

In this chapter, we'll traverse the vast plains of the hunter-gatherer's world. We'll learn how they viewed food as not just a source of sustenance, but as a critical aspect of their broader lifestyle that included physical activity, restorative sleep, stress management, and strong community bonds. These interconnected aspects of life were all vital to our ancestors' survival and robust health.

Our aim is to provide an illuminating view of the Paleo blueprint, allowing us to draw insights and wisdom that we can incorporate into our own lives. It's about understanding that our bodies are wonderfully complex systems that have been shaped by millions of years of evolution, and they function best when nourished and cared for in a manner that is congruent with their evolutionary design.

This chapter is divided into the following enlightening sections:

The Paleo Green Feast

I. Principles of the Paleo Diet

The Paleo diet is rooted in the idea that our bodies are better suited to the foods our ancestors consumed during the Paleolithic era, a period that spans from approximately 2.5 million to 10,000 years ago. This idea is based on the concept of evolutionary discordance, which suggests that our modern diets, influenced heavily by post-agricultural revolution foods, are at odds with our bodies' genetic predispositions. The Paleo diet aims to realign our food choices with our biological needs for optimal health.

So, what exactly does a Paleo diet encompass? Here are the key principles:

1. Whole, Unprocessed Foods: The Paleo diet emphasizes eating foods in their most natural state. This means choosing fresh fruits and vegetables, lean meats, seafood, nuts, and seeds, while avoiding processed foods laden with artificial additives and preservatives.

2. High Protein Intake: Our Paleolithic ancestors' diet was high in protein, obtained primarily from lean meats and seafood. Modern interpretations of the Paleo diet advocate for a higher protein intake than what is typically found in a standard Western diet.

3. Low Carbohydrate Intake and Low Glycemic Index Foods: The Paleo diet suggests a lower carbohydrate intake, especially from refined sugars and grains. It encourages consumption of non-starchy vegetables and fruits, which have a low glycemic index, meaning they are less likely to cause rapid spikes in blood sugar.

4. Healthy Fats: The Paleo diet promotes the consumption of healthy fats from sources such as avocados, nuts and seeds, olives, and certain oils like olive and coconut oil. It also emphasizes the importance of balancing omega-3 to omega-6 fatty acid ratios by incorporating more omega-3-rich foods, like fatty fish.

5. Exclusion of Certain Food Groups: The Paleo diet recommends avoiding dairy products, legumes, and grains. The rationale behind this exclusion is that these food groups were introduced into the human diet after the advent of agriculture and may cause digestive or inflammatory issues for some people.

6. Emphasis on Food Quality: Whenever possible, the Paleo diet advocates choosing grass-fed, pasture-raised meats, wild-caught fish, and organic fruits and vegetables to reduce exposure to hormones, antibiotics, and pesticides common in conventionally farmed products.

These principles serve as a blueprint, a guide to help you make food choices that align with the dietary patterns of our Paleolithic ancestors. However, it's important to remember that the Paleo diet should not be overly dogmatic or restrictive. It's about finding a balance and making informed decisions that best serve your health, lifestyle, and personal preferences.

In the next section, we'll delve into the potential benefits of the Paleo diet, providing a clearer picture of why these principles can contribute to better health.

II. Benefits of the Paleo Diet

Embracing the principles of the Paleo diet can yield a multitude of health benefits, thanks to its focus on nutrient-dense, whole foods and its elimination of heavily processed ones. The Paleo diet is not just about returning to our roots; it's a scientific approach to nutrition designed to optimize our health by aligning our diets with our genetic requirements. Here are some of the key benefits:

1. Weight Management: Many people turn to the Paleo diet for its potential to aid in weight loss and management. The diet's high protein content can increase satiety, reducing overall calorie intake. Moreover, by excluding processed foods, sugars, and grains, the diet naturally lowers the intake of high-calorie, low-nutrient foods.

2. Improved Glucose Control: The Paleo diet's focus on low-glycemic foods can help regulate blood sugar levels. This is particularly beneficial for individuals with insulin resistance, prediabetes, or diabetes. It's also useful for anyone looking to maintain stable energy levels throughout the day.

3. Enhanced Cardiovascular Health: The Paleo diet promotes heart health in several ways. Its emphasis on lean proteins, healthy fats, fruits, vegetables, and elimination of processed foods can help reduce risk factors for heart disease, such as high cholesterol and high blood pressure.

4. Reduced Inflammation: Chronic inflammation is a key contributor to many modern diseases. The Paleo diet, rich in omega-3 fatty acids and antioxidants, and low in inflammatory omega-6 fats, can help balance the body's inflammatory response.

5. Improved Gut Health: By eliminating foods that are potentially irritating to the gut (like dairy and grains) and focusing on nutrient-dense foods, the Paleo diet may promote a healthier gut microbiome, enhancing digestion and nutrient absorption.

6. Higher Nutrient Density: The Paleo diet, filled with fruits, vegetables, lean meats, and healthy fats, offers a wide range of essential vitamins, minerals, and antioxidants. The absence of processed foods also means you avoid harmful additives and preservatives.

7. Better Sleep and Energy Levels: By regulating blood sugar levels and providing a steady supply of energy through high-quality nutrients, the Paleo diet can help improve sleep quality and daytime energy levels.

8. Enhanced Physical Performance: Many athletes are drawn to the Paleo diet for its ability to support physical performance and recovery. Its high protein content aids muscle recovery and growth, while its balance of macronutrients supports sustained energy.

While the Paleo diet offers many potential benefits, it's important to remember that everyone's body responds differently to dietary changes. The degree to which you experience these benefits may depend on your starting point, your adherence to the diet, and your individual genetic make-up and lifestyle. It's always a good idea to consult with a healthcare provider or a dietitian before embarking on significant dietary changes.

III. Challenges of the Paleo Diet—and Overcoming Them

While the Paleo diet has many benefits, like any lifestyle change, it comes with its own set of challenges. It's important to understand these potential obstacles to successfully incorporate the principles of the Paleo diet into your life.

1. Restrictiveness and Social Situations: The Paleo diet can be seen as restrictive, as it excludes certain food groups such as dairy, grains, and legumes. This restriction can make it difficult to adhere to the diet, especially during social events or when dining out.

Solution: Flexibility is key. A Paleo lifestyle doesn't mean you can never enjoy non-Paleo foods. Consider adopting an 80/20 approach, where 80% of your diet adheres to Paleo principles and the remaining 20% allows for flexibility. This balance can make the diet more sustainable and enjoyable.

2. Potential Nutrient Deficiencies: By excluding dairy, grains, and legumes, there is a risk of missing out on essential nutrients like calcium, Vitamin D, and certain B vitamins.

Solution: Be sure to include a wide variety of foods within the Paleo framework to get a range of nutrients. For instance, leafy greens, almonds, and salmon are excellent sources of calcium. Mushrooms and eggs can provide Vitamin D, and liver and seafood can supply B vitamins. A well-formulated Paleo diet can be nutritionally complete.

3. Cost and Accessibility: High-quality meats, seafood, and organic fruits and vegetables can be more expensive than processed foods, which may make the Paleo diet seem financially inaccessible to some.

Solution: There are several strategies to make the Paleo diet more affordable. Buying in bulk, choosing seasonal produce, prioritizing which foods to buy organic, and opting for less expensive cuts of meat can help manage costs. Remember, the goal is not perfection, but progress.

4. Time and Convenience: Preparing meals from scratch takes more time than eating pre-packaged foods or dining out.

Solution: Meal planning and prepping can be helpful in managing time. Consider setting aside a few hours each week to prepare meals in advance. Also, keep a stock of Paleo-friendly snacks on hand for when you need a quick bite.

5. Adapting to a Lower Carb Intake: Some people may experience symptoms like fatigue, headaches, or mood swings as their bodies adjust to fewer carbs, commonly referred to as the "keto flu".

Solution: Ensure a balanced intake of macronutrients to prevent drastic drops in carb consumption. Gradually reduce your carb intake, and be sure to drink plenty of water and get enough electrolytes.

The challenges of transitioning to a Paleo diet shouldn't deter you from exploring its potential benefits. By understanding these challenges and knowing how to address them, you're better equipped to make the Paleo lifestyle work for you.

As we conclude this chapter, it's clear that the Paleo diet is not merely a fad or a quick fix to our health woes. Instead, it offers a comprehensive lifestyle approach, one that champions the consumption of whole, nutrient-dense foods and excludes heavily processed ones. The Paleo diet calls us to revert to our ancestral roots, aligning our nutritional intake with our evolutionary biology to potentially stave off modern diseases, enhance our physical performance, and boost our overall health.

The Paleo diet extends far beyond the realm of what we place on our dinner plates. It implores us to examine the interconnectedness between diet, physical activity, sleep, stress management, and community engagement—elements that were critical to our ancestors' survival and well-being. By embracing these lifestyle factors, we're not just following a diet; we're entering a profound and transformative journey toward optimal health.

Yet, it's crucial to acknowledge that embarking on the Paleo journey is not without its challenges. It demands significant changes to our food choices, some of which may seem restrictive or overwhelming at first glance. Nevertheless, as we've discussed in this chapter, these challenges are not insurmountable. They can be managed with flexibility, planning, and an open mindset that values progress over perfection. A well-implemented Paleo diet can provide a broad spectrum of nutrients, promote satiety, and fit within a budget.

However, the Paleo diet is not a one-size-fits-all solution. Every person's genetic makeup, health status, lifestyle, and personal preferences play a vital role in determining how they can best integrate the principles of the Paleo diet into their lives. As such, it's crucial to adapt and personalize the Paleo approach according to your unique needs and circumstances. And always remember to seek advice from healthcare professionals when making significant dietary changes, especially if you have existing health conditions.

As we wrap up this chapter and look forward to the next, we'll explore an exciting convergence—a fusion of the Paleo principles with a plant-based approach. This combination forms the basis of *The Caveman's Green Table,* a dietary philosophy that promotes the consumption of lean proteins in alignment with a diverse array of plant-based foods. By embracing this balanced approach, we can enjoy the best of both worlds, fostering a sustainable and diverse dietary regimen that can revolutionize men's health.

Remember, the goal is not to emulate the caveman's diet in its entirety but to adapt its beneficial principles to our modern lives. It's about appreciating the wisdom inherent in our evolutionary biology and using this understanding to make informed, health-promoting dietary choices. As we proceed, may we all find inspiration in our ancestors' resilience and adaptability and channel those qualities in our pursuit of optimal health.

Chapter 3

Unraveling the Green Table—Exploring the Fundamentals of Plant-Based Nutrition

As we turn over a new leaf, delving into the world of plant-based nutrition, the color of our table begins to change. From the reds, browns, and whites of the Paleo diet, we now add vibrant greens, deep purples, and bright oranges. Welcome to the Green Table, where plants take center stage, not as mere sides or accompaniments, but as the stars of our dietary intake.

The Green Table is not about discarding our Paleo principles; it's about complementing them with the wealth of nutrients that plant-based foods offer. It's about finding a sustainable, harmonious balance between animal and plant foods—a balance that serves our health, our planet, and our fellow creatures.

This chapter seeks to unravel the fundamentals of plant-based nutrition. But before we proceed, it's essential to clarify a common misconception: "plant-based" does not necessarily mean "vegan" or "vegetarian." While these diets are indeed plant-based, the term "plant-based" encompasses a broader spectrum. It refers to a dietary approach that prioritizes plant foods—without entirely excluding animal-derived products. It's about adjusting the proportions on our plate, shifting the balance *in favor of* plant foods.

The Paleo Green Feast

By exploring plant-based nutrition, we aim to tap into the immense potential of plants in boosting our health, disease resistance, and longevity. The Green Table isn't just about adding more salads to our diet; it's about discovering the myriad ways in which we can incorporate plant foods into our daily lives, reaping the vast array of nutrients they offer.

In this chapter, we'll delve into the different types of plant-based diets and their respective merits. We'll explore the nutritional value of plant foods, shining a spotlight on their diverse vitamin, mineral, fiber, and phytonutrient content. We'll also tackle some common concerns about plant-based nutrition, such as protein adequacy and vitamin B12 intake.

Moreover, we'll examine the scientific evidence supporting plant-based diets in preventing and managing chronic diseases, enhancing gut health, and supporting mental well-being. We'll also discuss the environmental implications of our dietary choices, elucidating how shifting towards a plant-based diet can contribute to a more sustainable and equitable food system.

As we embark on this journey, we invite you to keep an open mind, to question conventional dietary norms, and to embrace the potential of plant-based foods in enriching your health. Whether you're a seasoned plant-based eater or someone just starting to explore this avenue, this chapter will provide you with a deeper understanding and appreciation of plant-based nutrition.

So, let's pull up a chair, grab our forks, and delve into the flavorful, colorful, and nutrition-packed world of the Green Table.

This chapter is divided into the following enlightening sections:

I. Plant-Based Diets Defined: From Veganism to Flexitarianism

A plant-based diet, as the name suggests, is a diet centered around plant foods. This broad term encompasses a variety of dietary approaches, all sharing the common principle of emphasizing plants while differing in their inclusion or exclusion of animal-derived foods. Let's delve into the key types of plant-based diets and understand their distinctive characteristics:

1. Vegan Diet: The most restrictive form of plant-based diet is the vegan diet, which excludes all animal-derived products. This includes meat, poultry, fish, dairy, eggs, and even honey. A well-planned vegan diet can be nutritionally complete, packed with a wealth of vitamins, minerals, and other vital nutrients. However, certain nutrients like Vitamin B12, which is naturally found only in animal-derived foods, must be obtained through fortified foods or supplements.

2. Vegetarian Diet: Vegetarian diets exclude meat, poultry, and fish but allow dairy products and eggs. Within this category, there are further classifications such as lacto-vegetarians (consume dairy but not eggs), ovo-vegetarians (consume eggs but not dairy), and lacto-ovo vegetarians (consume both eggs and dairy).

3. Pescatarian Diet: Pescatarians are essentially vegetarians who also consume fish and other seafood. This diet offers the benefits of plant-based eating while adding the nutritional value of seafood, rich in omega-3 fatty acids and high-quality protein.

4. Flexitarian or Semi-Vegetarian Diet: Flexitarianism is a more flexible approach to plant-based eating. Flexitarians primarily consume a plant-based diet but occasionally include meat, poultry, fish, dairy, and eggs. The frequency and quantity of animal-derived foods consumed can vary based on personal preference. The flexitarian approach recognizes the health benefits of plant-based diets while allowing for flexibility to accommodate individual preferences, social situations, and cultural practices.

Understanding these various forms of plant-based diets can help you decide which approach aligns best with your lifestyle, ethical beliefs, and health goals. It's important to note that no matter which type of plant-based diet you choose, the key to nutritional adequacy is diversity. Consuming a wide variety of fruits, vegetables, grains, legumes, nuts, and seeds ensures a broad spectrum of nutrients, promoting optimal health.

In the next section, we will delve into the powerhouse of nutrients provided by plant foods, illuminating how a plant-centric diet can satisfy our nutritional needs and promote robust health.

II. The Powerhouse of Nutrients: Understanding the Nutritional Value of Plant Foods

The Paleo Green Feast

Plant foods, ranging from fruits, vegetables, and legumes to whole grains, nuts, and seeds, are nutrition powerhouses. They provide a host of essential nutrients required for optimal health. Let's delve into the rich tapestry of nutritional value that plant foods offer:

1. Macronutrients in Plant Foods:

Carbohydrates: Plants are the primary source of carbohydrates, which are our bodies' preferred source of energy. Whole plant foods like fruits, vegetables, legumes, and whole grains provide complex carbohydrates, which are digested slowly, keeping us feeling satiated and helping regulate blood sugar levels.

Protein: Contrary to popular belief, plant foods can be excellent sources of protein. Legumes, whole grains, nuts, seeds, and even some vegetables can contribute significantly to our daily protein needs.

Fats: While plants are typically low in fat, certain plant foods like avocados, nuts, seeds, and olives provide healthy fats, including monounsaturated and polyunsaturated fats, which are crucial for brain function, hormone production, and the absorption of fat-soluble vitamins.

2. Micronutrients in Plant Foods:

Vitamins and Minerals: Plant foods are rich in vitamins and minerals. For instance, citrus fruits are known for their high vitamin C content, dark leafy greens are packed with vitamins A and K, and legumes are excellent sources of iron and zinc.

Phytonutrients: These are natural compounds found in plant foods that have various health benefits. They include antioxidants, which protect our bodies from damage by free radicals, and other compounds that have been linked to reduced risk of chronic diseases.

3. Fiber: Plant foods are the only natural source of dietary fiber. Fiber plays an essential role in digestive health, helps control blood sugar levels, aids in weight management, and has been linked to lower risks of heart disease and certain types of cancer.

As you can see, plant foods provide a diverse range of nutrients, contributing to all aspects of our health. But it's not just about the individual nutrients. The real power of plant foods lies in the way these nutrients interact and work together within our bodies, creating a synergy that promotes health and well-being far beyond what each nutrient could do alone.

In the next sections, we'll tackle some common concerns about plant-based diets, starting with the hotly debated topic of protein. We'll debunk some myths and provide practical tips on ensuring adequate protein intake when adhering to a plant-based diet.

III. Protein and Plant-Based Diets: Dispelling the Myths

One of the most enduring myths about plant-based diets is the belief that they can't provide enough protein. This concern, although well-meaning, is often based on misunderstandings about protein requirements and the protein content of plant foods. Let's break down the myths and shed light on the truth about protein and plant-based diets.

1. Understanding Protein Needs: The Recommended Dietary Allowance (RDA) for protein for adult men and women is 46–56 grams per day, respectively, depending on age and level of physical activity. It's important to remember that this is not a minimal requirement, but an amount that covers the needs of 97–98% of healthy individuals. Most people, regardless of their diet, tend to consume more than this recommended amount.

2. Protein Quality and Complementarity: A common concern about plant proteins is their quality, specifically, their amino acid profile. Proteins are made up of amino acids, some of which are termed "essential" because our bodies cannot produce them, and we must obtain them from our diet. While it's true that most plant proteins are "incomplete," meaning they lack, or are low, in one or more essential amino acids, this does not pose a problem as long as a variety of plant foods are consumed. This concept, known as protein complementarity, ensures that you get all the essential amino acids over the course of the day, even if not from a single food source.

3. Plant Sources of Protein: Many plant foods are rich in protein. For instance, legumes (beans, lentils, chickpeas, etc.), whole grains (quinoa, brown rice, oats), soy products (tofu, tempeh, edamame), and nuts and seeds all contain substantial amounts of protein. Even vegetables and fruits contribute to our daily protein intake.

4. Practical Tips for Meeting Protein Needs: Incorporating a variety of protein-rich plant foods in your meals throughout the day can ensure you meet your protein needs on a plant-based diet. You might start your day with a smoothie made with plant-based protein powder or hemp seeds, enjoy a quinoa salad for lunch, snack on nuts and seeds in the afternoon, and have a lentil stew for dinner.

In conclusion, it is entirely feasible to meet your protein needs on a plant-based diet. Not only that, but the wide array of plant proteins brings along with them an abundance of other nutrients, including fiber, vitamins, minerals, and beneficial plant compounds, offering a nutritional package that extends beyond just protein.

In the following section, we will address another nutrient of concern in plant-based diets—Vitamin B12—and discuss its sources and the importance of adequate intake.

IV. Vitamin B12 and Plant-Based Diets: Meeting Your Needs

Vitamin B12, also known as cobalamin, plays a crucial role in our health. It's essential for the formation of red blood cells, neurological function, and DNA synthesis. However, Vitamin B12 is one of the few nutrients that cannot be readily found in plant foods, raising legitimate concerns about B12 adequacy in strictly plant-based or vegan diets.

1. The Importance of Vitamin B12: B12 deficiency can lead to serious health problems, including megaloblastic anemia and neurological disorders. It's crucial, especially for those following a strictly plant-based diet, to ensure an adequate intake of this vital nutrient.

2. Sources of Vitamin B12 in Plant-Based Diets: While B12 is naturally found in animal foods, there are several ways those on plant-based diets can meet their B12 needs:

Fortified Foods: Many plant-based foods are fortified with B12, including plant milks, breakfast cereals, meat substitutes, and some types of nutritional yeast. Reading food labels can help you identify which products have been fortified with B12.

Supplements: Given the potential challenges of obtaining enough B12 from fortified foods alone, a B12 supplement is often recommended for those on a strictly plant-based diet. B12 supplements are available in various forms, including tablets, capsules, and liquid drops.

3. How Much B12 Do You Need? The recommended dietary allowance (RDA) for adults is 2.4 micrograms (mcg) per day. However, the body's ability to absorb B12 decreases with age, and some people may require higher amounts. It's advisable to discuss your B12 needs with a healthcare provider or a dietitian specializing in plant-based nutrition.

4. Regular B12 Status Check: Given the vital role of B12 and the potential health implications of deficiency, it's advisable for those on a strictly plant-based diet to have their B12 status regularly checked. This is typically done through a simple blood test.

In conclusion, while obtaining adequate B12 on a plant-based diet requires some attention and planning, it is entirely achievable through a combination of fortified foods, supplements, and regular monitoring of B12 status. By taking these steps, you can enjoy the numerous benefits of plant-based eating while ensuring your B12 needs are met.

As we conclude Chapter 3, it's important to step back and appreciate the journey we've embarked upon in exploring the fundamentals of plant-based nutrition. From defining what plant-based diets encompass to discussing the nutrients that plant foods offer, we are taking a deep dive into the realm of plant-powered eating. And as we've uncovered, this isn't a diet that's lacking—it's one that's rich and vibrant, filled with a variety of nutrient-dense foods.

The Paleo Green Feast

Understanding the various forms of plant-based diets, including vegan, vegetarian, pescatarian, and flexitarian, underscores that there's not a one-size-fits-all approach to plant-based eating. These diets exist on a spectrum, allowing you to choose the approach that best aligns with your lifestyle, ethical beliefs, and health goals. There's room for flexibility, and the power to shape your diet in a way that *feels good* and *works* for you.

Diving into the nutritional value of plant foods, we've seen the power of plants to provide a wealth of essential nutrients. From macronutrients like carbohydrates, proteins, and fats, to micronutrients such as vitamins, minerals, antioxidants, and phytonutrients, to the dietary fiber exclusive to plant foods—plant-based diets offer a nutritional package that's diverse and comprehensive. We've also addressed and debunked common misconceptions, such as the myth that plant-based diets are inherently deficient in protein. By including a variety of plant foods, you can meet your protein needs and benefit from the array of other nutrients these foods provide.

Additionally, we've discussed the importance of Vitamin B12 in plant-based diets. Though B12 is not readily available from plant foods, this doesn't mean that individuals following plant-based diets are doomed to deficiency! With the availability of fortified foods and supplements, coupled with regular B12 status checks, individuals can ensure they meet their B12 needs and maintain optimal health.

Throughout this chapter, we've emphasized the importance of variety in a plant-based diet. By eating a diverse range of plant foods, you can ensure you're meeting your nutritional needs and enjoying the full spectrum of flavors, textures, and colors that plant foods offer. After all, part of the appeal of a plant-based diet lies in its diversity and the joy of exploring new foods and recipes.

As we've surveyed the Green Table, we've come to see it not as a diet of restriction, but one of abundance. It's a way of eating that celebrates the bounty of plant foods, emphasizing their taste, their beauty, and their ability to nourish our bodies and support our health. And as we'll see in the next chapter, merging these plant-based principles with the Paleo, or caveman's, approach to eating can create a balanced, sustainable, and health-promoting dietary pattern.

In closing, it's worth remembering that dietary choices are deeply personal and can be influenced by various factors, including culture, taste preferences, health goals, and ethical beliefs. The aim of this book isn't to advocate for a specific dietary approach, but to provide information and guidance to help you make informed choices about your diet. Whether you choose to go fully plant-based, adopt a flexitarian approach, or incorporate plant-based principles into a Paleo diet, the goal is the same—to promote health, respect the planet, and enjoy the food you eat.

Chapter 4

The Perfect Blend—Merging Paleo and Plant-Based Diets for Optimal Men's Health

The Perfect Blend—Merging Paleo and Plant-Based Diets for Optimal Men's Health is a unique turning point in our journey towards understanding and implementing a healthier lifestyle. After discussing the Paleo and plant-based diets separately, we are now at the juncture where we'll explore how these two approaches can be blended harmoniously. This chapter serves as the nucleus of our book, combining the strengths of both dietary philosophies to create a comprehensive and personalized dietary blueprint for men's health.

The path to optimal health doesn't involve a singular, one-size-fits-all diet. Instead, it requires the fusion of different dietary principles, allowing for personalization, flexibility, and diversity in food choices. By merging Paleo principles with plant-based nutrition, we can craft a diet that honors our evolutionary heritage while acknowledging the power of plant foods for health and sustainability. A diet that can be individualized to your needs, preferences, and lifestyle, ensuring that it is not just nutritionally adequate, but also enjoyable and sustainable for the long term.

This chapter will delve into the details of merging the Paleo and plant-based diets. We will start with the common ground between the two approaches, highlighting areas of alignment that might surprise you. For instance, both Paleo and plant-based diets emphasize whole, minimally processed foods, shunning additives, refined sugars, and unhealthy fats. Both approaches also advocate for a high intake of fruits and vegetables, recognizing their essential role in providing vital nutrients and promoting overall health.

The Paleo Green Feast

From there, we'll discuss how to incorporate the strengths of the Paleo diet—such as its emphasis on lean proteins, avoidance of highly processed foods, and focus on foods our ancestors would have eaten—into a predominantly plant-based dietary pattern. We'll delve into practical strategies for ensuring adequate protein and nutrient intake, discuss the role of healthy fats, and provide guidance on choosing whole, unprocessed plant foods that align with both Paleo and plant-based principles.

The integration of these two dietary approaches doesn't just enhance the diet's nutritional quality; it also broadens its potential health benefits. A combination of Paleo and plant-based principles could provide a dietary approach that supports heart health, helps maintain a healthy weight, fosters gut health, enhances physical performance, and potentially reduces the risk of chronic diseases. Furthermore, this combined approach respects our planet by promoting sustainable food choices.

The aim is to equip you with the knowledge, strategies, and confidence to create a balanced, nutrient-rich diet that aligns with your health goals and lifestyle. A diet that combines the best of *The Caveman's Green Table*, paving the way for optimal men's health.

In essence, this chapter seeks to bridge the gap between two seemingly distinct dietary philosophies. While each diet has its unique principles, they also have overlapping elements that we can leverage to enhance nutritional quality and optimize health. We'll discuss how to strike a balance between the nutrient-dense, unprocessed foods emphasized in the Paleo diet and the diverse, fiber-rich, and antioxidant-packed foods that form the core of plant-based diets.

This synthesis of dietary philosophies isn't just about meeting your nutrient needs; it's about crafting a way of eating that is sustainable, enjoyable, and beneficial for both personal health—and planetary health. We are moving beyond the concept of diet as a mere means of obtaining nutrients, to diet as a means of promoting health, preventing disease, enhancing longevity, and respecting our environment.

As we embark on this journey of merging Paleo and plant-based principles, let's keep in mind that the goal is not perfection, but progress. It's about making small, sustainable changes that add up over time, not about completely overhauling your diet overnight. It's about finding joy in the process, savoring the taste of whole, nutritious foods, and celebrating the power of diet in your life.

This chapter can be divided into the following sections:

I. Common Ground: Highlighting the Similarities between Paleo and Plant-Based Diets

In this section, we will explore the common ground shared by the Paleo and plant-based diets, highlighting areas of alignment that might surprise you. Although these two dietary approaches may seem distinct at first glance, they have more in common than meets the eye.

Both the Paleo and plant-based diets emphasize the consumption of whole, minimally processed foods. They encourage steering clear of additives, refined sugars, unhealthy fats, and artificial ingredients that have become prevalent in the modern food landscape. By prioritizing whole foods, both diets recognize the importance of obtaining nutrients in their most natural and bioavailable forms.

Furthermore, both diets advocate for a high intake of fruits and vegetables. Fruits and vegetables are nutritional powerhouses, packed with vitamins, minerals, antioxidants, and fiber. They offer a wide range of health benefits, including reduced risk of chronic diseases, improved digestion, and enhanced immune function. The shared emphasis on plant foods underscores the significance of incorporating these nutrient-dense options into our daily eating habits.

Another aspect that aligns these diets is the recognition of the harmful effects of highly processed foods. Processed foods often contain excessive amounts of added sugars, unhealthy fats, and artificial additives. By prioritizing whole, unprocessed foods, both the Paleo and plant-based diets promote a return to natural, nourishing sources of nutrition, steering away from the detrimental effects of processed foods on our health.

The Paleo Green Feast

Despite their differing stances on animal-derived foods, the Paleo and plant-based diets converge on the importance of sourcing high-quality, ethically raised animal products. The Paleo diet emphasizes consuming grass-fed meats, wild-caught fish, and pasture-raised poultry, recognizing the superior nutritional profile and environmental sustainability of these choices. Similarly, the plant-based diet encourages opting for organic, free-range, and ethically sourced animal products for those who include them in their diet. This shared emphasis on quality sourcing reflects the broader understanding that the health and welfare of animals are interconnected with our own well-being.

By highlighting the common ground between the Paleo and plant-based diets, we can begin to see the potential for integration and synergy. Recognizing these shared principles allows us to create a dietary approach that embraces the strengths of both philosophies. We can harness the nutrient density and ancestral wisdom of the Paleo diet while capitalizing on the health-promoting properties, sustainability, and diversity of plant-based nutrition.

II. Incorporating Paleo Principles into a Plant-Based Diet

In this section, we will delve into practical strategies for incorporating Paleo principles into a predominantly plant-based diet. By doing so, we can tap into the strengths of the Paleo approach while maintaining the focus on plant foods that form the core of a plant-based diet.

One key aspect of the Paleo diet is the emphasis on lean proteins. While plant-based diets are often associated with an abundance of carbohydrates, it's essential to remember that incorporating adequate protein is crucial for optimal health. To merge the Paleo and plant-based approaches, consider including plant-based protein sources such as legumes (beans, lentils, and chickpeas), tofu, tempeh, seitan, edamame, and plant-based protein powders. These options provide a range of essential amino acids necessary for protein synthesis and overall health.

In addition to lean proteins, the Paleo diet encourages the consumption of whole, unprocessed foods. This aligns with the principles of a plant-based diet that emphasizes whole grains, fruits, vegetables, nuts, and seeds. By focusing on these unrefined and minimally processed options, you can ensure a higher intake of nutrients, fiber, and phytochemicals.

Another important aspect of the Paleo diet is the avoidance of highly processed and refined foods. This principle can be integrated into a plant-based diet by scrutinizing food labels and choosing products that are minimally processed, contain whole food ingredients, and are free from additives, preservatives, and artificial sweeteners. Prioritizing whole foods allows you to maximize the nutritional value of your meals while minimizing the consumption of potentially harmful substances.

III. Ensuring Adequate Protein and Nutrient Intake

One common concern when adopting a plant-based or merged dietary approach is ensuring adequate protein and nutrient intake. To address this, it's important to emphasize the consumption of a wide variety of plant foods to provide a diverse array of nutrients.

In addition to plant-based proteins, such as legumes and tofu, it's essential to include whole grains, nuts, seeds, and vegetables that contribute to your protein needs. Incorporating these protein-rich plant foods into your meals throughout the day will help ensure you meet your daily protein requirements.

Moreover, by focusing on nutrient-dense plant foods, you can ensure adequate intake of essential vitamins and minerals. Leafy green vegetables, cruciferous vegetables, berries, citrus fruits, whole grains, and nuts and seeds are excellent sources of vitamins, minerals, and antioxidants. By consuming a wide variety of these plant foods, you can obtain the necessary micronutrients for overall health and well-being.

To optimize nutrient absorption, consider food combinations that enhance nutrient bioavailability. For example, pairing foods rich in vitamin C with plant-based iron sources can enhance iron absorption. Combining sources of healthy fats, such as avocados, nuts, and seeds, with fat-soluble vitamins from vegetables, can enhance the absorption of these vitamins.

The Paleo Green Feast

Additionally, monitoring your nutrient intake and considering supplementation can be beneficial, especially for nutrients that are more challenging to obtain from plant-based sources. Vitamins such as B12 and D, as well as minerals like zinc and iodine, may require supplementation or careful attention to fortified foods to ensure adequacy.

By focusing on a diverse range of plant foods, combining protein sources, and monitoring your nutrient intake, you can create a merged diet that meets your nutritional needs and supports optimal health.

IV. The Role of Healthy Fats in a Merged Diet

Healthy fats are an essential component of a well-balanced diet, providing energy, supporting hormone production, aiding in nutrient absorption, and promoting overall health. In this section, we will discuss the role of healthy fats in a merged Paleo and plant-based diet and explore sources that align with both approaches.

The Paleo diet emphasizes the consumption of quality fats, such as those found in avocados, nuts, seeds, olive oil, coconut oil, and fatty fish like salmon. These fats are rich in monounsaturated and polyunsaturated fats, including omega-3 fatty acids, which have been associated with numerous health benefits, including reduced inflammation, improved heart health, and enhanced brain function.

When merging the Paleo and plant-based diets, you can continue incorporating these healthy fat sources. Avocados, for instance, are a versatile and nutrient-dense food that can be used in salads, spreads, or even as a substitute for butter or mayonnaise. Nuts and seeds, such as almonds, walnuts, chia seeds, and flaxseeds, can be added to meals, snacks, or used as toppings for salads or smoothies. Extra-virgin olive oil and coconut oil can be used in cooking, salad dressings, or homemade sauces.

Moreover, certain plant foods, such as olives, coconuts, and durian, can provide plant-based sources of saturated fats, which are also present in animal-derived foods. However, it's important to consume these in moderation and prioritize the consumption of unsaturated fats as the primary source of dietary fats.

By incorporating healthy fats into your merged diet, you can enhance the flavor, satiety, and nutrient profile of your meals while reaping the benefits associated with these essential nutrients.

V. Choosing Whole, Unprocessed Plant Foods

The foundation of both the Paleo and plant-based diets is the focus on whole, unprocessed foods. In this section, we will provide guidance on selecting plant-based foods that align with both dietary approaches, ensuring that your meals are nutrient-dense and support optimal health.

When choosing plant foods, prioritize whole grains, such as quinoa, brown rice, oats, and whole wheat, which provide a range of nutrients, including fiber, B vitamins, and minerals. Choose intact grains rather than highly processed options like white flour or white rice, as these can have a higher glycemic impact and fewer nutrients.

Vegetables and fruits are key components of a merged diet. Aim to include a variety of colors, as each hue represents a unique set of beneficial compounds. Dark leafy greens, cruciferous vegetables (such as broccoli and kale), colorful peppers, berries, and citrus fruits are all excellent choices. These plant foods are rich in vitamins, minerals, antioxidants, and fiber, supporting overall health and well-being.

Legumes, such as beans, lentils, and chickpeas, are versatile plant-based protein sources that are also high in fiber and other important nutrients. Including legumes in your merged diet can provide a significant nutritional boost while offering a range of flavors and textures.

Nuts and seeds are another vital component of a merged diet. They are packed with healthy fats, protein, fiber, vitamins, minerals, and antioxidants. Almonds, walnuts, sunflower seeds, chia seeds, and flaxseeds can be incorporated into meals, snacks, or used as toppings for salads, cereals, or yogurt.

To further optimize your diet, minimize the consumption of processed and refined plant-based products. These include foods such as vegan burgers, sausages, and other heavily processed meat substitutes. While they can be enjoyed in moderation, it's important to focus on whole, minimally processed plant foods as the foundation of your merged diet.

The Paleo Green Feast

By prioritizing whole, unprocessed plant foods, you can maximize nutrient density, minimize exposure to potentially harmful additives, and enjoy the full spectrum of flavors and textures that nature has to offer.

VI. Health Benefits of the Merged Approach

In this section, we will delve into the potential health benefits of merging Paleo and plant-based principles. By combining the strengths of these two dietary approaches, you can unlock a range of benefits that contribute to optimal men's health.

One of the primary advantages of the merged approach is the promotion of heart health. The emphasis on whole, unprocessed foods in both the Paleo and plant-based diets helps reduce the consumption of unhealthy fats, added sugars, and refined carbohydrates. By incorporating lean proteins, healthy fats, and a variety of fruits, vegetables, and whole grains, the merged diet can help maintain healthy cholesterol levels, blood pressure, and body weight, all of which are crucial for cardiovascular well-being.

Weight management is another area where the merged approach can be beneficial. The emphasis on nutrient-dense, fiber-rich plant foods can help promote feelings of fullness and satiety, making it easier to control calorie intake and manage weight. Additionally, the inclusion of lean proteins and healthy fats provides sustained energy and supports muscle maintenance, which is essential for a healthy body composition.

Gut health is another area of focus in the merged approach. The abundance of fiber from plant foods promotes a healthy gut microbiome, supporting digestion, nutrient absorption, and overall gut function. Additionally, the inclusion of fermented foods, such as sauerkraut, kimchi, and tempeh, which are aligned with both Paleo and plant-based principles, can introduce beneficial probiotics and further enhance gut health.

The merged approach also has the potential to enhance physical performance. By providing a diverse range of nutrients, including proteins for muscle repair and growth, carbohydrates for energy, and antioxidants for recovery and immune support, this dietary blend can optimize athletic performance and support an active lifestyle.

Furthermore, the merged approach may have potential benefits in reducing the risk of chronic diseases. By prioritizing whole, unprocessed foods and incorporating a variety of plant foods, you can ensure a high intake of antioxidants, phytochemicals, and other bioactive compounds that have been associated with reduced inflammation, improved immune function, and decreased risk of chronic conditions such as heart disease, certain cancers, and diabetes.

VII. Personalizing the Perfect Blend

In this section, we emphasize the importance of personalization in the merged approach. Each person has unique dietary needs, preferences, and goals, and it's essential to tailor the diet accordingly.

Personalization starts with considering your individual protein requirements. Some individuals may have higher protein needs due to factors such as age, activity level, or specific health conditions. Assessing and adjusting protein intake accordingly ensures that you meet your individual needs while maintaining the balance between plant-based and lean animal protein sources.

Additionally, it's crucial to consider any specific dietary restrictions or intolerances you may have. For instance, if you are lactose-intolerant or have a gluten sensitivity, you can adapt the merged approach to exclude or substitute the respective foods while still maintaining the overall principles of the diet.

Lifestyle factors should also be taken into account when personalizing the merged approach. Factors such as work schedule, availability of cooking facilities, and cultural preferences can influence your dietary choices. By considering these factors, you can create a merged diet that suits your lifestyle and makes it easier to adhere to the principles.

It's also important to listen to your body and make adjustments as needed. Pay attention to how different foods make you feel and adapt your diet accordingly. If certain plant foods don't agree with you or if you feel the need for more variety, be open to exploring different options and finding the right balance that supports your well-being.

The Paleo Green Feast

VIII. Embracing a Sustainable and Health-Promoting Dietary Pattern

As we conclude chapter 4, it's crucial to emphasize the overarching goal of the merged approach—creating a sustainable and health-promoting dietary pattern. By merging Paleo and plant-based principles, we strive to harness the strengths of both approaches to enhance not only our personal health but also the health of the planet.

A merged diet that emphasizes plant foods reduces the environmental footprint associated with the production of animal-based foods. By incorporating more plant-based protein sources and minimizing the consumption of animal products, we contribute to environmental sustainability, conserve natural resources, and reduce greenhouse gas emissions.

Furthermore, a merged diet that prioritizes whole, unprocessed foods aligns with the principles of mindful eating and fosters a deeper connection with the food we consume. It encourages us to be more conscious of our food choices, savor the flavors and textures of wholesome ingredients, and appreciate the nourishment and vitality that food provides.

As we conclude this chapter, it's crucial to reflect on the wealth of information and guidance we have explored to create a comprehensive dietary blueprint that optimizes men's health.

Throughout this chapter, we have highlighted the common ground shared by the Paleo and plant-based diets, revealing surprising areas of alignment. Both approaches prioritize whole, unprocessed foods, emphasize the importance of fruits and vegetables, and discourage the consumption of additives, refined sugars, and unhealthy fats. By recognizing these shared principles, we have laid the foundation for merging the best of both approaches into a powerful dietary blend.

Incorporating Paleo principles into a predominantly plant-based diet has been a focal point of this chapter. We have explored practical strategies for incorporating lean proteins, such as legumes, tofu, and plant-based protein sources, into plant-based meals. By emphasizing whole, unprocessed foods and avoiding highly refined and processed options, we have embraced the principles of the Paleo diet while maintaining the focus on plant-based nutrition.

Ensuring adequate protein and nutrient intake has been another critical aspect of merging the two diets. By combining a variety of plant-based protein sources, including legumes, whole grains, nuts, and seeds, we can meet our protein needs while reaping the benefits of the array of nutrients present in these plant foods. Emphasizing a diverse range of fruits, vegetables, whole grains, and healthy fats provides us with a wide spectrum of vitamins, minerals, antioxidants, and phytochemicals essential for optimal health.

We have also explored the role of healthy fats in a merged diet, recognizing their significance in supporting overall well-being. By incorporating sources such as avocados, nuts, seeds, and quality oils, we have embraced the importance of healthy fats while maintaining the balance between plant-based and lean animal protein sources. These fats not only provide essential nutrients but also enhance the flavor and satiety of meals.

Choosing whole, unprocessed plant foods has been a central theme in our discussion. By prioritizing whole grains, vegetables, fruits, legumes, nuts, and seeds, we have maximized nutrient density and minimized exposure to harmful additives and refined ingredients. This selection of plant foods provides us with a wide range of vitamins, minerals, fiber, and antioxidants, promoting overall health and vitality.

As we conclude chapter 4, it's important to recognize the potential health benefits of the merged approach. By merging the strengths of the Paleo and plant-based diets, we can promote heart health, support weight management, enhance gut health, improve physical performance, and reduce the risk of chronic diseases. The merged approach not only focuses on personal health but also contributes to sustainability and environmental stewardship by reducing the reliance on animal-based foods and embracing the abundance of plant-based options.

Personalization has been a key aspect of our exploration, acknowledging that each individual has unique dietary needs, preferences, and goals. By considering protein requirements, dietary restrictions or intolerances, lifestyle factors, and personal feedback from our bodies, we can tailor the merged approach to suit our individuality. This empowers us to create a sustainable and health-promoting dietary pattern that is enjoyable, manageable, and supportive of our overall well-being.

The Paleo Green Feast

As we move forward in our journey, the merged approach offers us a transformative way of eating—one that celebrates the best of both worlds. By merging the ancestral wisdom of the Paleo diet with the vibrancy and nourishment of plant-based nutrition, we unlock a dietary blueprint that supports optimal men's health. The synergy of these two approaches creates a sustainable, diverse, and nutrient-rich diet that honors our evolutionary heritage, fosters personal well-being, and contributes to the health of our planet.

Vesla Ekstedt

Chapter 5

Protein Paradox—Addressing the Common Myths and Realities of Protein Sources

Protein is often hailed as the cornerstone of a healthy diet, playing a crucial role in supporting various bodily functions and maintaining overall well-being. However, misconceptions and myths surrounding protein sources can distort our understanding of this essential macronutrient. In Chapter 5, "Protein Paradox—Addressing the Common Myths and Realities of Protein Sources," we dive into the intricate world of protein and debunk the misconceptions that surround its sources. By exploring the realities and dispelling the myths, we aim to provide a comprehensive understanding of protein sources and guide informed choices that optimize our health.

There is a prevailing myth that consuming animal-derived sources, such as meat, poultry, and dairy, is the only way to obtain sufficient protein. This belief overlooks the fact that protein is abundantly available in a wide range of plant-based sources as well. Throughout this chapter, we will unravel the protein paradox, challenging the notion that animal sources are inherently superior to plant sources in terms of protein quality and bioavailability.

Contrary to popular belief, plant-based sources can provide all the essential amino acids our bodies need for optimal protein synthesis. While it is true that some plant proteins may be lower in certain essential amino acids, combining different plant protein sources can easily address these limitations and ensure a complete amino acid profile. The concept of protein complementation allows us to maximize the nutritional value of plant proteins and dispel the myth that they are inferior to animal proteins.

Protein is not solely about amino acids. Plant-based proteins come bundled with a host of additional nutrients, fiber, antioxidants, vitamins, minerals, and beneficial phytochemicals. These components contribute to the overall health-promoting properties of plant proteins and play a significant role in disease prevention and overall well-being. By shifting our focus from protein quantity alone to the nutritional package as a whole, we can appreciate the unique benefits that plant-based protein sources offer.

Understanding our individual protein requirements based on factors such as age, sex, activity level, and specific health conditions is crucial for maintaining a balanced diet. The myth that more protein is always better is dispelled as we explore the realities of protein requirements. Striking the right balance and consuming the optimal amount of protein for our individual needs is key to supporting our health and well-being.

Chapter 5 will take us on a journey through the diverse landscape of protein sources, catering to different dietary preferences and needs. From animal-based sources such as lean meats, poultry, fish, and dairy to plant-based sources like legumes, tofu, tempeh, seitan, nuts, and seeds, we will uncover the nutritional profiles, benefits, and considerations of various protein sources. By embracing the nutritional diversity of both animal and plant-based proteins, we can make informed decisions that align with our health, ethical values, and environmental concerns.

This chapter is divided into the following enlightening sections:

I. The Protein Myth

Protein is a macronutrient that has been widely celebrated for its essential role in nourishing the body. However, one of the most prevalent myths surrounding protein is the belief that animal-derived sources are the *sole* means of obtaining sufficient protein. This myth has been perpetuated by societal norms, cultural traditions, and the influence of the food industry. In this section, we will challenge this misconception and shed light on the realities of protein sources.

The Paleo Green Feast

First and foremost, it is important to acknowledge that protein is abundant in a diverse array of plant-based sources. Contrary to the belief that animal proteins are inherently *superior,* plant proteins can provide all the essential amino acids needed for optimal health and protein synthesis. While it is true that certain plant proteins may be lower in specific essential amino acids, such as lysine or methionine, the concept of protein complementation can easily address this. By combining different plant protein sources, we can create a complete amino acid profile that matches or even surpasses the protein quality of animal sources.

Furthermore, the notion that animal proteins are superior is often based on the concept of protein digestibility and bioavailability. While animal proteins are indeed highly digestible, plant proteins can also be easily digested and absorbed by the body when consumed in adequate amounts. Factors such as food processing, cooking methods, and individual variations can influence the digestibility of both animal and plant proteins. It is crucial to consider the overall nutritional package and not solely focus on protein quantity or digestibility when evaluating protein sources.

Another important consideration is the potential health implications associated with the consumption of animal-based protein sources. High intake of red and processed meats has been linked to an increased risk of certain health conditions, including heart disease, certain cancers, and type 2 diabetes. On the other hand, plant-based proteins come bundled with an array of beneficial nutrients, fiber, antioxidants, and phytochemicals that have been associated with reduced inflammation, improved heart health, and a decreased risk of chronic diseases. By shifting the focus from animal protein-centric diets to a more balanced and diverse protein intake that includes plant sources, we can reap the benefits of a wider range of nutrients and potentially reduce the risk of certain health issues.

Addressing the protein myth involves dispelling the notion that animal sources are the sole path to meeting protein needs. By embracing the abundance of plant-based protein sources and understanding the principles of protein complementation, we can enjoy a varied and nutritionally rich diet that supports optimal health while aligning with ethical considerations and sustainability concerns.

II. The Reality of Plant Protein

In this section, we will delve into the reality of plant protein and explore the numerous benefits and considerations associated with incorporating plant-based protein sources into our diets. By understanding the unique qualities of plant proteins, we can dispel myths surrounding their inferiority and appreciate their potential to support optimal health.

Complete Protein Profile through Complementation:

While it is true that some plant proteins may be lower in certain essential amino acids compared to animal proteins, the concept of protein complementation offers a solution. By combining different plant protein sources, we can create a complete amino acid profile that provides all the essential amino acids our bodies require for protein synthesis. For example, grains are typically lower in lysine but higher in methionine, while legumes are lower in methionine but higher in lysine. Combining these two sources in a meal, such as beans and rice or lentils and quinoa, ensures a balanced amino acid profile. By understanding the principles of protein complementation, we can meet our protein needs while enjoying the diverse flavors and textures that plant-based foods offer.

Nutrient-Dense and Fiber-Rich:

Plant-based protein sources come bundled with a plethora of additional nutrients, fiber, antioxidants, vitamins, minerals, and phytochemicals that contribute to overall health and well-being. Unlike many animal proteins, which can be higher in saturated fat and cholesterol, plant proteins are generally low in saturated fat and devoid of cholesterol. Additionally, plant-based protein sources are often rich in dietary fiber, which promotes healthy digestion, helps maintain a healthy weight, and supports heart health. The fiber content of plant proteins contributes to a feeling of fullness, aiding in portion control and weight management.

Reduced Risk of Chronic Diseases:

The Paleo Green Feast

Studies consistently indicate that a plant-based diet, which includes a variety of plant proteins, is associated with a reduced risk of chronic diseases. Research has linked higher consumption of plant proteins with a lower risk of heart disease, hypertension, certain types of cancer, and type 2 diabetes. Plant proteins are typically low in saturated fat and high in unsaturated fats, which promote heart health and help lower LDL (bad) cholesterol levels. The presence of antioxidants, phytochemicals, and other bioactive compounds in plant-based protein sources further contribute to disease prevention and the promotion of overall well-being.

Environmental and Ethical Considerations:

Choosing plant-based protein sources aligns with ethical and environmental considerations. Animal agriculture is associated with significant greenhouse gas emissions, land and water degradation, and the consumption of resources. By shifting our protein intake towards plant-based sources, we can reduce our ecological footprint, contribute to sustainable food systems, and promote animal welfare. Plant proteins offer an opportunity to support a more sustainable and compassionate approach to human nutrition.

Variety and Culinary Exploration:

Incorporating plant proteins into our diets opens up a world of culinary possibilities and encourages exploration of diverse flavors and cuisines. Plant-based proteins such as legumes, tofu, tempeh, seitan, nuts, and seeds can be prepared in countless ways, offering versatility and creativity in the kitchen. From hearty lentil stews to protein-packed veggie burgers and nutrient-rich smoothies, plant-based protein sources allow for exciting and nutritious meal options.

By understanding the reality of plant protein, we can appreciate its nutritional value, health benefits, and the role it plays in creating a sustainable and balanced diet. Embracing plant proteins as a vital component of our meals not only supports our health but also addresses ethical and environmental concerns.

The following sections will explore protein requirements, provide guidance on selecting and incorporating different protein sources, and highlight the importance of a well-rounded and personalized approach to protein consumption. Through this exploration, we can make informed decisions about protein sources that align with our individual needs, preferences, and values while optimizing our health and well-being.

III. Beyond the Amino Acids

In this section, we will delve into the additional benefits and considerations associated with plant-based protein sources, going beyond their amino acid content. Plant proteins come bundled with a rich array of nutrients, fiber, antioxidants, vitamins, minerals, and phytochemicals that contribute to overall health and well-being. By understanding these extra components, we can appreciate the holistic advantages of incorporating plant-based protein sources into our diets.

Fiber-Rich Nutritional Powerhouses:

One of the standout features of plant-based protein sources is their high fiber content. Dietary fiber plays a crucial role in maintaining a healthy digestive system, promoting regular bowel movements, and supporting gut health. Plant proteins, such as legumes, whole grains, nuts, and seeds, are excellent sources of dietary fiber. The fiber in these foods adds bulk to our meals, providing a feeling of fullness and satiety, which can aid in weight management and portion control. Additionally, dietary fiber acts as a prebiotic, fueling the growth of beneficial gut bacteria and supporting a healthy gut microbiome. A robust gut microbiome is linked to various health benefits, including improved immune function and reduced risk of certain diseases.

Antioxidants and Phytochemicals:

The Paleo Green Feast

Plant-based protein sources are rich in antioxidants and phytochemicals, which are bioactive compounds that provide numerous health benefits. Antioxidants help protect our cells from damage caused by harmful free radicals, potentially reducing the risk of chronic diseases such as heart disease, cancer, and neurodegenerative disorders. Phytochemicals, found exclusively in plant foods, have been linked to various health-promoting effects, including anti-inflammatory and anti-cancer properties. Different plant-based protein sources offer a variety of unique antioxidants and phytochemicals, such as flavonoids, carotenoids, and polyphenols, each with its own specific health benefits.

Vitamins and Minerals:

Plant-based protein sources are abundant in essential vitamins and minerals that support various bodily functions. Legumes, for example, are excellent sources of folate, iron, magnesium, and potassium. Nuts and seeds provide essential minerals like zinc, selenium, and copper, as well as vitamin E and B vitamins. Whole grains contribute to our intake of B vitamins, including thiamin, niacin, and riboflavin, as well as minerals such as manganese and phosphorus. By incorporating a diverse range of plant-based protein sources, we can ensure a rich supply of essential micronutrients necessary for optimal health and well-being.

Reduced Inflammatory Potential:

Plant proteins have been associated with a reduced inflammatory potential compared to animal proteins. Chronic inflammation is a contributing factor to many health conditions, including heart disease, diabetes, and autoimmune disorders. Plant-based protein sources, particularly those rich in antioxidants and phytochemicals, can help combat inflammation and promote a more balanced and anti-inflammatory environment in the body. By prioritizing plant proteins, we can potentially lower our risk of chronic inflammation-related diseases and support overall health.

Weight Management and Metabolic Health:

The nutrient density and fiber content of plant-based protein sources contribute to their potential role in weight management and metabolic health. High-fiber plant proteins promote feelings of fullness and satiety, which can help regulate appetite and reduce overeating. Additionally, the low saturated fat content of many plant proteins supports heart health and can contribute to better weight management. By incorporating plant-based proteins into a balanced diet, we can support weight loss or maintenance goals and enhance overall metabolic health.

IV. Navigating Protein Requirements

In this section, we will explore the realities of protein requirements and provide guidance on how to navigate them effectively. While it is important to consume an adequate amount of protein, it is equally crucial to understand that more protein is not always better. Optimal protein intake varies depending on individual factors such as age, sex, activity level, and specific health conditions. By understanding and meeting our unique protein requirements, we can maintain a balanced diet and support our overall health and well-being.

Assessing Protein Needs:

Determining your protein needs begins with considering several key factors. These include your age, as protein requirements may vary during different life stages, such as growth periods or older adulthood. Sex can also influence protein needs, as males typically require more protein due to higher muscle mass and different metabolic rates. Activity level plays a significant role, as those engaged in intense physical activity or strength training may require higher protein intake to support muscle repair and growth. Lastly, specific health conditions or goals, such as pregnancy, breastfeeding, or recovery from illness or injury, may necessitate adjustments to protein intake.

Recommended Protein Intake:

The Paleo Green Feast

Protein recommendations can vary depending on the source and guidelines consulted. However, general guidelines suggest that adults should aim for a range of 0.8 to 1 gram of protein per kilogram of body weight per day. This range provides an estimate of the minimum protein needed to support basic bodily functions and prevent deficiencies. For those engaged in regular physical activity or seeking muscle gain, protein intake may be higher, ranging from 1.2 to 2 grams per kilogram of body weight per day. Consulting with a healthcare professional or registered dietitian can help determine the appropriate protein intake for you, based on your individual circumstances.

Balancing Protein Sources:

When considering protein intake, it is essential to balance both animal and plant-based protein sources. Animal proteins, such as lean meats, poultry, fish, and dairy products, provide complete protein profiles and are often rich in essential nutrients like iron, zinc, and vitamin B12. However, they can also be higher in saturated fat and cholesterol. On the other hand, plant-based proteins like legumes, tofu, tempeh, and quinoa offer a wealth of fiber, antioxidants, and phytochemicals. By combining both animal and plant-based protein sources, we can create a well-rounded and nutritionally diverse diet that meets our protein needs while considering other health factors.

Personalization and Individual Differences:

It is important to recognize that individual protein requirements may differ based on personal factors, genetics, and health conditions. Some individuals may have higher protein needs due to factors like increased muscle mass, metabolic disorders, or specific dietary restrictions. Personalization also involves considering other aspects of one's diet and lifestyle, such as carbohydrate and fat intake, overall calorie balance, and exercise habits. By taking a holistic approach to nutrition and considering individual differences, we can better tailor our protein intake to support our unique needs and goals.

V. Protein Sources for Optimal Health

In this section, we will explore a range of protein sources that contribute to optimal health. Both animal-based and plant-based protein sources offer various benefits and considerations, allowing individuals to select options that align with their preferences, dietary restrictions, and ethical choices. By incorporating a variety of protein sources, we can meet our protein requirements while enjoying a diverse and nutritious diet.

Animal-Based Protein Sources:

Animal-based protein sources include lean meats, poultry, fish, eggs, and dairy products. These sources provide high-quality protein with a complete amino acid profile and are rich in essential nutrients like iron, zinc, and vitamin B12. It is important to choose lean cuts of meat, poultry without the skin, and low-fat dairy options to minimize saturated fat intake. For individuals who choose to consume animal-based protein sources, selecting sustainable and ethically sourced options is encouraged.

Plant-Based Protein Sources:

Plant-based protein sources offer a wide variety of options that are both nutritious and sustainable. Legumes, such as beans, lentils, and chickpeas, are excellent sources of protein, fiber, and essential minerals. Tofu, tempeh, and other soy products provide complete protein profiles and are versatile ingredients in many cuisines. Whole grains, such as quinoa, amaranth, and brown rice, also contribute to protein intake while offering complex carbohydrates and fiber. Nuts, seeds, and nut butters are protein-rich additions to meals and snacks. Additionally, certain vegetables like spinach, broccoli, and Brussels sprouts contain notable amounts of protein. By incorporating a variety of plant-based protein sources, individuals can obtain the necessary amino acids and enjoy the benefits of a plant-centric diet.

Combining Protein Sources:

The Paleo Green Feast

Combining different protein sources can further enhance the nutritional value and diversity of one's diet. For example, mixing legumes with whole grains, such as rice and beans, creates a complete amino acid profile. Combining different plant-based protein sources throughout the day ensures a range of nutrients and flavors. Additionally, incorporating plant-based protein sources as complementary components in dishes featuring animal proteins can provide a balanced and varied approach to protein intake.

Considerations for Specific Dietary Needs:

Individuals with dietary restrictions or preferences, such as those following vegetarian, vegan, or gluten-free diets, can still meet their protein requirements by carefully selecting appropriate protein sources. Plant-based protein options like legumes, tofu, tempeh, and quinoa are particularly valuable for those enjoying a vegetarian or vegan lifestyle. Additionally, individuals with gluten intolerance or celiac disease can choose gluten-free grains, such as amaranth or quinoa, to meet their protein needs while avoiding gluten-containing sources.

By incorporating a diverse range of protein sources, balancing animal and plant-based options, and considering individual needs and preferences, individuals can meet their protein requirements while enjoying a nutritionally rich and sustainable diet. The key is to personalize protein intake, considering factors such as age, sex, activity level, and health conditions, to optimize health and well-being. Consulting with a registered dietitian or healthcare professional can provide further guidance on individualized protein needs and sources.

By debunking the myth that animal-derived sources are the sole means of obtaining sufficient protein, we have embraced the reality that plant-based protein sources offer a wealth of benefits for optimal health. As we conclude this chapter, let us reflect on the key takeaways and the implications they have for our overall well-being.

One of the fundamental insights gained from this chapter is the concept of protein complementation. By combining different plant protein sources, we can create a complete amino acid profile that matches or exceeds the protein quality of animal sources. This realization challenges the myth that plant proteins are inferior and underscores the versatility and nutrient density of plant-based protein options. Embracing protein complementation opens up a world of culinary possibilities, allowing us to enjoy a diverse range of flavors, textures, and nutrient profiles while meeting our protein needs.

Beyond the amino acids themselves, plant-based protein sources offer a plethora of additional benefits. The high fiber content of these sources contributes to healthy digestion, weight management, and a reduced risk of chronic diseases. Fiber-rich plant proteins promote feelings of fullness and satiety, aiding in portion control and supporting overall gut health. The presence of antioxidants, phytochemicals, vitamins, and minerals in plant proteins further enhances their health-promoting properties, potentially reducing inflammation and supporting various bodily functions.

By incorporating plant-based proteins, we not only benefit our individual health but also contribute to ethical and environmental considerations. Plant proteins are more sustainable and have a lower environmental impact compared to animal proteins. Choosing plant-based options allows us to reduce greenhouse gas emissions, conserve natural resources, and promote animal welfare. This aligns with the growing social awareness of the need for sustainable and compassionate food choices, making plant proteins a very appealing option for those concerned about the broader implications of their dietary decisions.

Navigating protein requirements is a critical aspect of maintaining a balanced diet. It is essential to recognize that protein needs vary based on individual factors such as age, sex, activity level, and specific health conditions. By understanding our unique requirements and personalizing our protein intake, we can ensure that we meet our individual needs while considering other aspects of our diet and lifestyle. Balancing both animal and plant-based protein sources allows us to create a well-rounded and nutritionally diverse approach to protein consumption.

Chapter 6

Power Foods—Embracing the Bounty of Nature for Energy and Vitality

"Power Foods—Embracing the Bounty of Nature for Energy and Vitality," takes us on a journey through the realm of nutrition-rich foods that have the potential to fuel our bodies and invigorate our lives. Power foods are the superheroes of the culinary world, bursting with essential nutrients, antioxidants, and other bioactive compounds that offer numerous health benefits. By incorporating these nutrient-dense foods into our diets, we can enhance our energy levels, support our overall well-being, and unlock the full potential of our bodies.

In a world inundated with processed and unhealthy food choices, it is crucial to rediscover the power of whole, natural foods that are abundantly available in nature. These foods, whether sourced from plants, animals, or a combination of both, have a transformative effect on our health and vitality. They provide a symphony of nutrients that work synergistically to nourish our bodies, boost our immune systems, and promote optimal functioning of our organs and systems.

The notion of power foods goes beyond mere sustenance. These foods have been celebrated for centuries in various cultures for their medicinal properties and healing potential. From ancient Ayurvedic practices to traditional Chinese medicine, the power of certain foods to restore balance, improve longevity, and support vibrant health has long been recognized and revered. In this chapter, we will explore the science behind these power foods, unravel their benefits, and learn how to incorporate them into our daily lives.

The Paleo Green Feast

Power foods encompass a vast array of options, each with its unique profile of nutrients and health-promoting properties. We will explore nutrient-dense fruits and vegetables, vibrant herbs and spices, whole grains, lean proteins, and beneficial fats. By understanding the nutritional composition of these foods and their potential impact on our bodies, we can make informed choices that fuel us from within and provide the building blocks for a vibrant life.

In addition to their nutrient content, power foods are often packed with antioxidants and other bioactive compounds that protect our cells from damage caused by free radicals and oxidative stress. These compounds have anti-inflammatory properties and can potentially reduce the risk of chronic diseases such as heart disease, cancer, and neurodegenerative disorders. The vibrant colors, distinct flavors, and aromas of power foods are a testament to the presence of these potent compounds.

Moreover, power foods offer a natural and sustainable approach to nourishing our bodies. By prioritizing whole foods over the many processed and refined options, we reduce our intake of additives, preservatives, and artificial ingredients. Embracing power foods allows us to reconnect with nature, supporting local and seasonal produce, and reducing our carbon footprint. This sustainable approach to nutrition not only benefits our own well-being but also contributes to the health of our planet.

Throughout this chapter, we will explore the nutritional powerhouses that nature has provided and uncover the science behind their benefits. From the antioxidants in berries to the omega-3 fatty acids in fatty fish, we will delve into the unique properties of these foods and learn how to harness their potential for energy, vitality, and overall health.

As we journey through the world of power foods, let us embrace the abundance of nature's bounty and rediscover the incredible potential of these nutrient-dense gifts. By incorporating power foods into our daily lives, we can nourish our bodies, enhance our energy levels, and experience the vibrant health and vitality that we deserve. So, get ready to embark here on this exciting exploration of power foods and unlock the keys to a vibrant and nourished life.

Power Foods—Embracing the Bounty of Nature for Energy and Vitality can be divided into the following sections:

I. The Nutritional Powerhouses

In the realm of nutrition, some foods rise above the rest, earning the title of "power foods." These nutritional powerhouses are packed with an array of essential nutrients, antioxidants, and bioactive compounds that fuel our bodies and promote energy and vitality. In this section, we will explore the concept of power foods and delve into their significance in supporting our overall well-being.

Power foods are not mere staples in our diets; they are nutritional superheroes that provide a wide range of health benefits. These foods offer a symphony of vitamins, minerals, fiber, and phytochemicals that work synergistically to nourish our bodies and boost our immune systems. They play a vital role in providing the necessary building blocks for optimal functioning of our organs, supporting cellular health, and aiding in the repair and regeneration of tissues.

One of the key characteristics of power foods is their high nutrient density. Unlike empty-calorie foods that provide little nutritional value, power foods offer a wealth of essential nutrients in every bite. They are nature's way of delivering a concentrated dose of vitamins, minerals, and other vital compounds that our bodies need in order to thrive. By incorporating these foods into our diets, we can ensure that we are meeting our nutrient requirements and supporting our overall health.

Antioxidants are a crucial component of power foods, playing a vital role in protecting our cells from damage caused by free radicals. These unstable molecules can lead to oxidative stress, which has been linked to chronic diseases such as heart disease, cancer, and neurodegenerative disorders. Power foods are rich in antioxidants, which help neutralize free radicals and reduce the risk of cellular damage. The vibrant colors found in fruits, vegetables, and herbs are often a visual indicator of their antioxidant content.

The Paleo Green Feast

Bioactive compounds, another hallmark of power foods, go beyond basic nutrition to offer additional health benefits. These compounds have been extensively studied for their potential to reduce inflammation, support cardiovascular health, enhance immune function, and even protect against certain types of cancer. From polyphenols in berries to curcumin in turmeric, each power food contains its own unique combination of bioactive compounds that contribute to its health-promoting properties.

Embracing power foods means incorporating a diverse array of plant-based and animal-based options into our diets. Fruits and vegetables, with their vibrant colors and varied nutrient profiles, form the foundation of power foods. From leafy greens to cruciferous vegetables, each variety offers its own nutritional benefits. Whole grains, lean proteins, and beneficial fats also have their place among the nutritional powerhouses, providing essential macronutrients and micronutrients necessary for optimal health.

In addition to their nutritional prowess, power foods offer a sustainable and natural approach to nourishing our bodies. By choosing whole, unprocessed foods over their refined counterparts, we reduce our intake of additives, preservatives, and artificial ingredients. Embracing power foods allows us to reconnect with nature, supporting local and seasonal produce, and reducing our environmental impact. Choosing power foods is not only beneficial for our own well-being but also contributes to the health of our planet.

As we journey through the world of power foods, let us celebrate the diversity and abundance that nature has provided. By incorporating these nutritional powerhouses into our diets, we can fuel our bodies, support our immune systems, and experience the transformative effects of optimal nutrition. So, let us embrace the vibrant colors, the flavors, and the nourishment that power foods offer, and unlock the keys to enhanced energy and vitality.

II. Fruits and Vegetables: Nature's Nutritional Gems

In the world of power foods, few categories shine as brightly as fruits and vegetables. These vibrant, nutritional gems are packed with an abundance of essential vitamins, minerals, fiber, and phytochemicals that contribute to overall health and vitality. In this section, we will delve into the colorful realm of fruits and vegetables, exploring their unique nutritional profiles and the myriad health benefits they offer.

Nutrient Density and Variety:

Fruits and vegetables are unparalleled in their nutrient density, offering a treasure trove of essential vitamins and minerals that are vital for our well-being. From vitamin C in citrus fruits to potassium in bananas and folate in leafy greens, each fruit and vegetable brings its own nutritional profile to the table. Incorporating a diverse range of fruits and vegetables into our diets ensures that we receive a wide spectrum of nutrients, supporting our immune system, promoting healthy digestion, and fueling countless cellular processes in our bodies.

Antioxidant Powerhouses:
One of the standout features of many fruits and vegetables is their high antioxidant content. These powerful compounds play a crucial role in protecting our cells from oxidative damage caused by free radicals. Berries, such as blueberries, strawberries, and raspberries, are particularly rich in antioxidants, including anthocyanins and vitamin C. Leafy green vegetables like spinach and kale are packed with antioxidants such as lutein and zeaxanthin, which support eye health. The vibrant hues of fruits and vegetables often indicate their antioxidant potency, making them a feast for both the eyes and the rest of the body.

Fiber for Digestive Health:

Fruits and vegetables are excellent sources of dietary fiber, a nutrient that plays a vital role in supporting healthy digestion. Fiber adds bulk to our meals, promoting regular bowel movements and preventing constipation. It also provides a feeling of fullness, helping to control appetite and support weight management. The fiber in fruits and vegetables acts as a prebiotic, nourishing the beneficial bacteria in our gut and promoting a healthy gut microbiome. By including a variety of fruits and vegetables in our diets, we can support optimal digestive health and maintain a happy gut.

The Paleo Green Feast

Phytochemical Powerhouses:

In addition to their nutrient and fiber content, fruits and vegetables are rich in phytochemicals, bioactive compounds that offer a range of health benefits. These compounds include carotenoids, flavonoids, and polyphenols, among others, each with its unique properties. For example, the carotenoids lycopene in tomatoes and beta-carotene in carrots have been linked to a reduced risk of certain cancers and heart disease. Flavonoids, found in berries, citrus fruits, and apples, have anti-inflammatory and antioxidant effects. The phytochemicals in cruciferous vegetables, such as broccoli and cauliflower, have been associated with detoxification and cancer prevention. By incorporating a colorful array of fruits and vegetables, we can enjoy the benefits of these phytochemical powerhouses.

Culinary Versatility:

Fruits and vegetables offer endless culinary possibilities, adding color, flavor, and texture to our meals. From refreshing salads to flavorful stir-fries, vibrant smoothies to roasted vegetable medleys, the options are virtually limitless. Exploring different cooking methods, such as steaming, sautéing, or grilling, can enhance the flavors and nutritional profiles of these plant-based powerhouses. Adding herbs, spices, and healthy dressings further elevates the taste and nutritional value of fruits and vegetables, making them an enticing and satisfying part of our daily diet.

Incorporating a wide variety of fruits and vegetables into our diets is an essential step towards embracing the power of these nutritional gems. By savoring their vibrant colors, enjoying their unique flavors, and appreciating their countless health benefits, we can nourish our bodies and unleash its full potential. So, let us venture into the world of fruits and vegetables, relishing their abundance, and celebrating the natural wonders that they offer to support our well-being.

III. Herbs, Spices, and Culinary Delights: Flavorful Power Foods

In this section, we turn our attention to the world of herbs, spices, and culinary delights. These flavor-packed power foods not only add zest and aroma to our dishes but also offer an array of health benefits, including anti-inflammatory and antimicrobial properties. Let's explore the diverse and vibrant realm of herbs, spices, and other culinary delights and uncover their unique contributions to our well-being.

Antioxidant-Rich Herbs:

Herbs such as basil, oregano, thyme, rosemary, and parsley are not only bursting with flavor but also pack a powerful antioxidant punch. These culinary herbs contain a variety of beneficial compounds, including flavonoids, carotenoids, and phenolic acids, which have potent antioxidant and anti-inflammatory properties. The antioxidants in herbs help protect our cells from damage caused by free radicals, potentially reducing the risk of chronic diseases such as heart disease and certain types of cancer. Incorporating fresh or dried herbs into our cooking allows us to enhance the flavor of our dishes while reaping the health benefits they offer.

Spices for Flavor and Health:

Spices not only add depth and complexity to our culinary creations but also provide a host of health benefits. Turmeric, a bright yellow spice commonly used in Indian cuisine, contains a compound called curcumin, which has potent anti-inflammatory and antioxidant properties. Cinnamon has been shown to help regulate blood sugar levels and may improve insulin sensitivity. Ginger has long been used for its digestive and anti-inflammatory properties. Other spices like cumin, coriander, and paprika also contribute their unique flavors and health-promoting properties. Incorporating a variety of spices into our cooking not only enhances taste but also adds a touch of medicinal magic to our meals.

Culinary Delights with Health Benefits:

The Paleo Green Feast

Beyond herbs and spices, certain culinary delights have earned their place as power foods due to their exceptional nutritional profiles and health benefits. Garlic, for example, not only adds savory flavor to dishes but also possesses antimicrobial and immune-boosting properties. Onions, known for their pungent aroma, contain compounds that may help reduce inflammation and support heart health. Fermented foods like sauerkraut, kimchi, and yogurt provide beneficial bacteria, known as probiotics, that promote a healthy gut microbiome. These culinary delights add depth and complexity to our meals while nourishing our bodies from within.

Maximizing Flavor and Health:

To make the most of the health benefits offered by herbs, spices, and culinary delights, it is important to use them mindfully in our cooking. Opting for fresh herbs whenever possible ensures the maximum flavor and nutrient content. Experimenting with different spice blends and combinations can elevate the taste of our dishes while providing an array of health benefits. Embracing fermentation techniques or incorporating fermented foods into our meals allows us to enjoy their unique flavors and support a healthy gut microbiome. By harnessing the power of herbs, spices, and culinary delights, we can transform ordinary meals into extraordinary experiences for both our taste buds and our well-being.

Incorporating herbs, spices, and culinary delights into our daily cooking not only enhances the flavor and aroma of our meals but also offers a wealth of health benefits. From antioxidant-rich herbs to spice-filled wonders, these power foods contribute to our overall well-being while adding a touch of culinary delight to our lives. So, let us embark on a flavorful journey, exploring the world of herbs, spices, and culinary delights, and discovering new ways to infuse our meals with both taste and health benefits.

IV. Whole Grains: Nutritional Powerhouses for Sustained Energy

In this section, we turn our focus to whole grains, the nutritional powerhouses that form a fundamental part of a balanced diet. Whole grains are a rich source of complex carbohydrates, fiber, vitamins, minerals, and antioxidants that provide sustained energy and support various aspects of our health. Let's delve into the world of whole grains and uncover the remarkable benefits they offer.

Complex Carbohydrates for Energy:

Whole grains are excellent sources of complex carbohydrates, which serve as the primary fuel for our bodies. Unlike refined grains, which have been stripped of their bran and germ, whole grains retain these nutrient-rich components. This means that they release energy more slowly, providing a steady supply of fuel to keep us energized throughout the day. The complex carbohydrates in whole grains support brain function, fuel our muscles, and help regulate blood sugar levels.

Fiber for Digestive Health:

One of the standout features of whole grains is their high fiber content. Dietary fiber plays a crucial role in maintaining a healthy digestive system. It adds bulk to our stools, promoting regular bowel movements and preventing constipation. Additionally, fiber acts as a prebiotic, nourishing the beneficial bacteria in our gut and promoting a healthy gut microbiome. By including whole grains in our diet, we can support optimal digestive health and maintain a happy gut.

Nutrient-Rich Powerhouses:

Whole grains are not only a source of carbohydrates and fiber but also contain a wealth of essential vitamins, minerals, and antioxidants. They provide a range of B vitamins, including thiamin, niacin, and riboflavin, which are necessary for energy production and the proper functioning of our nervous system. Minerals such as magnesium, zinc, and iron are also found in abundance in whole grains, supporting various bodily processes, including immune function and oxygen transport.

Heart-Healthy Benefits:

Whole grains have been associated with a reduced risk of heart disease. Their fiber content helps lower cholesterol levels and maintain healthy blood pressure, reducing the risk of cardiovascular complications. The antioxidants and phytochemicals present in whole grains further contribute to their heart-protective effects. Incorporating whole grains into our diets as part of a balanced lifestyle can be a valuable step towards promoting heart health.

Variety of Whole Grains:

The world of whole grains is vast and diverse, offering an array of options to suit different tastes and culinary preferences. From quinoa and brown rice to oats, barley, and whole wheat, each grain has its unique flavor and nutritional profile. Experimenting with different grains allows us to explore new textures and tastes, making our meals exciting and nutritious. By incorporating a variety of whole grains into our diets, we can benefit from their collective nutrient power.

Incorporating whole grains into our meals is a delicious way to nourish our bodies and promote optimal health. Whether in the form of whole grain bread, brown rice, oatmeal, or quinoa, these nutritional powerhouses provide sustained energy, support digestive health, and contribute to our overall well-being. So, let us embrace the world of whole grains, savor their rich flavors, and experience the transformative impact they can have on our health.

V. Lean Proteins: Building Blocks for Health and Strength

In this section, we dive into the world of lean proteins, the building blocks that support our bodies' growth, repair, and overall health. Lean proteins are essential for muscle development, immune function, hormone production, and numerous other vital processes. Let's explore the remarkable benefits of incorporating lean proteins into our diets and discover the variety of sources that can help us achieve optimal health and strength.

Muscle Development and Repair:

Proteins are the fundamental components necessary for muscle development and repair. When we engage in physical activity or strength training, our muscles undergo stress and require proper nutrition to recover and grow stronger. Lean proteins, such as poultry, fish, legumes, and plant-based alternatives like tofu and tempeh, provide the essential amino acids needed for muscle protein synthesis. By incorporating lean proteins into our diets, we provide our bodies with the building blocks they need to support muscle development, repair damaged tissues, and optimize athletic performance.

Satiety and Weight Management:

Lean proteins play a crucial role in appetite regulation and weight management. Protein-rich foods have been shown to increase feelings of fullness and satiety, helping to control hunger and prevent overeating. Additionally, the thermic effect of protein—the energy required to digest and process protein—is higher than that of fats and carbohydrates. This means that our bodies burn more calories when metabolizing protein-rich foods, contributing to a higher metabolic rate. By incorporating lean proteins into our meals, we can support weight management goals and maintain a healthy body composition.

Essential Nutrients:

Lean proteins are not only valuable sources of protein but also provide essential nutrients necessary for overall health. Poultry and fish are rich in high-quality protein and are excellent sources of vitamins and minerals such as vitamin B12, iron, and zinc. Plant-based protein sources like legumes offer not only protein but also dietary fiber, folate, and potassium. By choosing a variety of lean protein sources, we can ensure that our bodies receive the full spectrum of nutrients needed to support optimal function and well-being.

Heart Health:

Incorporating lean proteins into our diets can have positive implications for heart health. Lean proteins, such as fish and poultry, are generally lower in saturated fat compared to red meats. Consuming less saturated fat is associated with a reduced risk of heart disease. Fatty fish, such as salmon and sardines, also provide omega-3 fatty acids, which have been shown to support heart health by reducing inflammation, improving blood lipid profiles, and supporting healthy blood pressure. By opting for lean protein sources and incorporating fatty fish into our diets, we can make heart-healthy choices that contribute to our overall well-being.

Plant-Based Protein Power:

Plant-based protein sources offer a wealth of benefits, both for our health and the planet. Legumes, such as beans, lentils, and chickpeas, are excellent sources of plant-based protein and provide additional benefits like dietary fiber and various vitamins and minerals. Tofu and tempeh, derived from soybeans, are complete protein sources that offer a versatile and sustainable alternative to animal-based proteins. By incorporating plant-based proteins into our diets, we can reduce our environmental footprint, support sustainable food systems, and enjoy the health benefits associated with plant-centric eating.

Personalization and Balance:

It is important to personalize protein intake based on individual factors such as age, sex, activity level, and specific health conditions. Consulting with a healthcare professional or registered dietitian can help determine the appropriate protein intake that meets individual needs and goals. Balancing protein sources, both animal-based and plant-based, allows us to create a well-rounded and nutritionally diverse diet. By embracing the variety and benefits of lean proteins, we can optimize our health, support our physical performance, and achieve a balanced approach to nutrition.

Lean proteins are the backbone of a well-rounded diet, providing essential amino acids, supporting muscle development and repair, and offering a wealth of nutrients necessary for overall health. Whether we choose poultry, fish, legumes, or plant-based alternatives, incorporating lean proteins into our meals allows us to fuel our bodies, manage weight effectively, and support long-term health goals. So, let us embrace the power of lean proteins, celebrate their diverse sources, and savor the nourishment they bring to our plates.

VI. Beneficial Fats: Nourishing the Mind and Body

In this section, we explore the world of beneficial fats, dispelling the myth that all fats are harmful. Beneficial fats play a crucial role in supporting brain health, providing essential fatty acids, aiding nutrient absorption, and promoting overall well-being. Let's delve into the realm of beneficial fats and uncover their remarkable contributions to nourishing both the mind and body.

Essential Fatty Acids:

Beneficial fats are a rich source of essential fatty acids, including omega-3 and omega-6 fatty acids, which are crucial for our health. Omega-3 fatty acids, found in fatty fish like salmon, mackerel, and sardines, as well as in flaxseeds and walnuts, have been shown to support brain function, reduce inflammation, and promote heart health. Omega-6 fatty acids, found in sources like sunflower seeds and soybean oil, also contribute to overall health but should be consumed in moderation to maintain a healthy balance with omega-3 fatty acids.

Brain Health and Cognitive Function:

The brain is largely composed of fats, and incorporating beneficial fats into our diets is vital for optimal brain health and cognitive function. Omega-3 fatty acids, in particular, play a critical role in brain development and function, supporting memory, concentration, and overall cognitive performance. Studies have linked higher omega-3 intake to a reduced risk of cognitive decline and neurodegenerative disorders like Alzheimer's disease. By including fatty fish, flaxseeds, chia seeds, and other sources of beneficial fats in our diets, we can nourish our minds and support long-term brain health.

Nutrient Absorption:

Beneficial fats play a crucial role in the absorption of fat-soluble vitamins, such as vitamins A, D, E, and K. These vitamins require the presence of fats for proper absorption and utilization in the body. By incorporating beneficial fats into meals that contain these vitamins, we enhance their bioavailability and ensure that our bodies can effectively utilize these essential nutrients. For example, pairing a spinach salad with a source of healthy fat, like olive oil, can maximize the absorption of fat-soluble vitamins present in the greens.

Heart-Healthy Benefits:

The Paleo Green Feast

Contrary to popular belief, consuming beneficial fats can actually promote heart health. Monounsaturated and polyunsaturated fats, found in sources like olive oil, avocados, nuts, and seeds, have been associated with a reduced risk of heart disease. These fats help lower LDL cholesterol levels (often referred to as "bad" cholesterol) and may improve overall blood lipid profiles. By incorporating these heart-healthy fats into our diets in moderation, we can make choices that support cardiovascular well-being.

Balancing Fats for Optimal Health:

While beneficial fats offer numerous health benefits, it is important to consume them in moderation and balance them with other macronutrients. Fats are calorie-dense, and excessive intake can lead to weight gain and other health issues. Striking a balance between beneficial fats, lean proteins, and complex carbohydrates ensures a well-rounded diet that supports overall health and well-being. Consulting with a healthcare professional or registered dietitian can provide personalized guidance on incorporating beneficial fats into a balanced meal plan.

Incorporating beneficial fats into our diets allows us to nourish our bodies, support brain health, and promote overall well-being. By choosing sources like fatty fish, avocados, nuts, and seeds, we can enjoy the diverse flavors and health benefits these fats offer. So, let us embrace the power of beneficial fats, prioritize their inclusion in our meals, and experience the transformative impact they have on our minds and bodies.

This chapter has taken us on a journey through the world of power foods, where we have explored the bountiful offerings of nature for energy and vitality. From nutrient-dense fruits and vegetables to flavorful herbs, spices, and culinary delights, and from the wholesome goodness of whole grains to the muscle-building properties of lean proteins and the nourishing benefits of beneficial fats, we have witnessed the remarkable potential of these foods to support our overall well-being.

Power foods are not merely ingredients on our plates; they are allies in our quest for a vibrant and nourished life. They provide us with a symphony of nutrients, antioxidants, and bioactive compounds that work harmoniously to fuel our bodies, protect our cells, support our immune systems, and optimize our organ functions. By embracing power foods, we empower ourselves to take charge of our health, both physically and mentally.

Throughout this chapter, we have unraveled the science behind power foods, discovering their nutritional profiles, health benefits, and culinary versatility. We have learned that power foods are not limited to a single category but encompass a diverse range of options, allowing us to tailor our choices to our individual preferences and dietary needs. Whether we choose plant-based power foods, animal-based sources, or a combination of both, the key lies in creating a well-rounded and personalized approach to nutrition.

Embracing power foods is not just a matter of individual human health but also has wider implications for the health of our planet. By prioritizing whole, natural foods and supporting sustainable food systems, we contribute to a more sustainable future on Earth. Choosing local and seasonal produce, reducing food waste, and opting for organic and environmentally friendly options aligns our dietary choices with our values, nurturing both our bodies and the Earth.

As we conclude this chapter, let us carry forward the knowledge and inspiration gained from the exploration of power foods. Let us embrace the vibrancy of fruits and vegetables, the aromatic allure of herbs and spices, the nourishing qualities of whole grains, the strength-building properties of lean proteins, and the brain-nurturing benefits of beneficial fats. Let us infuse our meals with creativity, variety, and mindfulness, savoring each bite as a celebration of both nourishment and pleasure.

By incorporating power foods into our daily lives, we can experience enhanced energy, vitality, and overall well-being. We can unleash the potential that lies within us and cultivate a deeper connection with the natural world. So, let us continue on this empowering journey, opening our minds and palates to the wonders of power foods, and embark on the pathway of nourishment, strength, and vibrant living.

Chapter 7

Thriving, not Just Surviving—Ensuring Adequate Nutrition While Balancing Paleo and Plant-Based Diets

In our quest for optimal health, we often find ourselves drawn towards specific dietary approaches that promise a multitude of benefits. The Paleo diet emphasizes a return to our ancestral roots, focusing on whole, unprocessed foods that mimic those consumed by our hunter-gatherer ancestors. On the other hand, the plant-based diet centers around the consumption of predominantly plant-derived foods, with a focus on fruits, vegetables, whole grains, and legumes. But what happens when we strive to find a *balance* between these two seemingly contrasting dietary philosophies?

Chapter 7 delves into the fascinating realm of harmonizing the Paleo and plant-based diets, exploring strategies to ensure adequate nutrition while embracing the best of both worlds. We aim to shed light on the potential challenges and misconceptions that arise when merging these two dietary approaches, providing practical guidance on how to thrive, not just survive, in this unique nutritional landscape.

The Paleo Green Feast

As we embark on this chapter, it is crucial to recognize that finding a balance between the Paleo and plant-based diets is a deeply personal journey. Our dietary choices should be guided by our individual needs, preferences, and health goals. By understanding the principles and key components of each diet, we can navigate this complex terrain with wisdom and intention, crafting a nutritional approach that promotes optimal health and vitality.

Throughout this chapter, we will explore the essential nutrients that may require special attention when merging the Paleo and plant-based diets. We will delve into the importance of protein, iron, calcium, omega-3 fatty acids, and vitamin B12, among others, and offer practical strategies to ensure their adequate intake. By addressing these nutritional considerations, we can thrive on a balanced Paleo and plant-based diet and enjoy the benefits of both approaches.

We will also debunk common misconceptions surrounding the Paleo and plant-based diets, highlighting the areas of overlap and dispelling the notion that these two dietary approaches are mutually exclusive. By focusing on whole, nutrient-dense foods, regardless of their origin, we can embrace the core principles of both diets and create a personalized eating plan that nourishes our bodies and supports our health goals.

In this chapter, we invite you to embark on a journey of discovery and self-reflection. We encourage you to approach the merging of the Paleo and plant-based diets with an open mind and a willingness to explore new culinary horizons. By seeking the guidance of healthcare professionals, registered dietitians, and incorporating evidence-based recommendations, we can ensure that our dietary choices are rooted in sound nutritional principles.

Ultimately, the goal is to thrive, not just survive, on a balanced Paleo and plant-based diet. By maintaining a diverse and nutrient-rich eating plan, we can optimize our health, support our well-being, and enjoy the benefits of both dietary approaches. So, let us embark on this exciting chapter, embracing the challenge of harmonizing these two philosophies, and paving the way for a sustainable, nourishing, and vibrant lifestyle.

I. Understanding the Paleo and Plant-Based Diets

Section 1 provides an in-depth further exploration of the Paleo and plant-based diets, outlining their principles, key components, and highlighting the areas of overlap and potential challenges when merging these two dietary approaches. By understanding the foundations of each diet, individuals can navigate the process of balancing the two and make informed choices that support their health and well-being.

1.1 Overview of the Paleo Diet:

The Paleo diet, also known as the Paleolithic or caveman diet, draws inspiration from the dietary patterns of our hunter-gatherer ancestors. It emphasizes whole, unprocessed foods that would have been available to early humans, including lean meats, fish, fruits, vegetables, nuts, and seeds. The diet excludes grains, legumes, dairy products, refined sugars, and processed foods.

The Paleo diet's primary focus is on consuming nutrient-dense foods that are minimally processed and free from additives. By adhering to the Paleo principles, individuals aim to fuel their bodies with foods that are believed to be more compatible with our genetic makeup, promoting optimal health and vitality.

1.2 Overview of the Plant-Based Diet:

The plant-based diet places a strong emphasis on foods derived from plants, including fruits, vegetables, whole grains, legumes, nuts, and seeds. It promotes the consumption of plant-derived foods as the primary source of nutrition, while minimizing or eliminating the consumption of animal-based products.

Plant-based diets can take various forms, ranging from vegetarianism (which excludes meat but may include animal by-products like dairy and eggs) to veganism (which excludes all animal-derived foods). The emphasis is on consuming whole, unprocessed plant foods that provide a rich array of vitamins, minerals, fiber, and phytochemicals.

1.3 Recognizing Areas of Overlap and Potential Challenges:

The Paleo Green Feast

While the Paleo and plant-based diets may seem divergent, there are areas of overlap that allow for a balanced approach. Both diets prioritize whole, unprocessed foods and encourage the consumption of fruits, vegetables, nuts, and seeds. They share a focus on nutrient density and the exclusion of processed and refined foods.

However, challenges arise when merging these two diets due to the differing views on certain food groups. The Paleo diet excludes grains and legumes, which are staple components of a plant-based diet. Conversely, the plant-based diet emphasizes the inclusion of grains, legumes, and sometimes soy-based products, which may not align with the Paleo principles.

Finding a balance between the Paleo and plant-based diets requires a thoughtful approach that considers individual preferences, health goals, and nutritional requirements. By understanding the principles and key components of each diet, individuals can navigate these challenges and create a personalized approach that combines the best aspects of both philosophies.

In the following sections of this chapter, we will delve deeper into the essential nutrients that may require special attention when merging the Paleo and plant-based diets. By addressing these nutritional considerations and debunking common misconceptions, we aim to provide practical guidance on how to thrive on a balanced Paleo and plant-based diet, ensuring optimal nutrition while reaping the benefits of both approaches.

II. Essential Nutrients for a Balanced Approach

Section 2 focuses on the essential nutrients that require special attention when balancing the Paleo and plant-based diets. By understanding these nutrients and implementing strategies to ensure their adequate intake, individuals can optimize their nutrition and support their overall health and well-being.

2.1 Protein: Incorporating Plant-Based Protein Sources

Protein is a vital macronutrient necessary for the growth, repair, and maintenance of tissues in the body. While animal-based sources are commonly associated with high-quality protein, individuals following a plant-based diet can obtain sufficient protein by incorporating a variety of plant-based sources. Legumes such as lentils, chickpeas, and beans are excellent sources of protein, as are soy products like tofu and tempeh. Additionally, whole grains, nuts, and seeds contribute to overall protein intake. By incorporating a combination of these plant-based protein sources, individuals can ensure they meet their protein needs while following a balanced Paleo and plant-based approach.

2.2 Iron: Addressing Sources and Absorption

Iron is essential for the transport of oxygen in the body and the formation of red blood cells. Plant-based sources of iron, known as non-heme iron, may be less readily absorbed by the body compared to the heme iron found in animal-based sources. To optimize iron absorption from plant-based sources, individuals can consume foods rich in vitamin C, such as citrus fruits or bell peppers, alongside iron-rich plant foods. Cooking in cast-iron cookware can also enhance iron levels in meals. Including iron-rich foods like dark leafy greens, legumes, fortified cereals, and dried fruits can help individuals meet their iron requirements while following a balanced Paleo and plant-based diet.

2.3 Calcium: Strategies without Dairy Products

Calcium is crucial for maintaining healthy bones, teeth, and overall body function. While dairy products are traditionally associated with calcium intake, individuals following a plant-based diet can obtain calcium from alternative sources. Dark leafy greens like kale and broccoli, fortified plant-based milk alternatives, tofu made with calcium sulfate, and calcium-set tempeh are excellent plant-based calcium sources. Additionally, incorporating foods fortified with calcium, such as certain cereals or juices, can contribute to overall calcium intake. By consciously choosing these calcium-rich plant-based options, individuals can ensure they meet their calcium needs while adhering to a balanced Paleo and plant-based diet.

2.4 Omega-3 Fatty Acids: Incorporating Plant-Based Sources

The Paleo Green Feast

Omega-3 fatty acids are essential fats that play a crucial role in brain health, heart health, and inflammation regulation. While fatty fish is a primary source of omega-3s in the Paleo diet, individuals following a plant-based approach can obtain these fats from plant sources. Flaxseeds, chia seeds, hemp seeds, and walnuts are excellent sources of plant-based omega-3 fatty acids. Incorporating these foods into the diet, either as whole seeds or as oils, can help individuals maintain adequate omega-3 levels while following a balanced Paleo and plant-based approach.

2.5 Vitamin B12: Supplementation or Fortified Foods

Vitamin B12 is primarily found in animal-based products, making it a potential challenge for individuals following a plant-based diet. Adequate vitamin B12 intake is crucial for nerve function, red blood cell production, and DNA synthesis. To ensure sufficient B12 levels, individuals can consider vitamin B12 supplementation or consuming fortified foods. Fortified plant-based milk alternatives, breakfast cereals, and nutritional yeast are common sources of plant-based fortified B12. Regular monitoring of B12 levels and consultation with healthcare professionals can guide individuals in determining the most suitable approach to meet their vitamin B12 needs.

By addressing these essential nutrients and implementing strategies to ensure their adequate intake, individuals can maintain a balanced Paleo and plant-based approach while optimizing their nutrition. With thoughtful meal planning and a focus on nutrient-dense plant-based sources, it is possible to thrive on a combined dietary approach. In the following sections, we will explore practical tips for balancing these diets, debunk common misconceptions, and emphasize the importance of seeking professional guidance for personalized advice on merging the Paleo and plant-based diets.

III. Practical Tips for Balancing the Diets

Section 3 offers practical tips and strategies for individuals seeking to balance the Paleo and plant-based diets. By implementing these recommendations, individuals can create well-rounded and nutritious meals that incorporate elements from both dietary approaches.

3.1 Meal Planning: Creating Balanced Meals

Meal planning is an essential tool for achieving a balanced approach. Start by designing meals that include a variety of colorful fruits and vegetables, whole grains, legumes, lean proteins (both plant-based and animal-based), and beneficial fats. Aim to fill your plate with a rainbow of plant foods, incorporating different textures and flavors. Experiment with different cooking methods and seasoning techniques to enhance the taste and appeal of your meals. By creating well-balanced and visually appealing plates, you can enjoy the best of both the Paleo and plant-based worlds.

3.2 Food Combining: Maximizing Nutrient Absorption

Combining different food groups strategically can enhance nutrient absorption and optimize digestion. For instance, combining iron-rich plant foods with vitamin C-rich foods can improve iron absorption. Pairing a spinach salad with citrus dressing or adding bell peppers to a lentil soup are examples of effective food combinations. Including a source of fat, such as avocado or olive oil, can also aid in the absorption of fat-soluble vitamins. By being mindful of food combinations, you can maximize nutrient availability and ensure you receive the full benefits of the foods you consume.

3.3 Cooking Techniques: Preserving Nutrients and Flavors

The cooking techniques you choose can impact the nutrient content and flavors of your meals. Adopt cooking methods that preserve the nutritional integrity of ingredients. Steaming, roasting, sautéing, and grilling are excellent cooking techniques that retain the natural flavors, colors, and nutrients of plant-based foods. Minimize the use of excessive oils and fats to maintain a balanced approach. By selecting cooking methods that enhance the sensory experience of your meals while preserving nutritional quality, you can create delicious and nutrient-dense dishes.

3.4 Supplementation: Bridging Nutritional Gaps

Supplementation can be a valuable tool to ensure adequate intake of specific nutrients that may be challenging to obtain solely through diet. For individuals following a balanced Paleo and plant-based diet, certain supplements may be beneficial, such as omega-3 fatty acids derived from algae for those not consuming fish or a reliable source of vitamin B12 for those on a strict plant-based approach. However, it is crucial to consult with healthcare professionals or registered dietitians to determine individual supplement needs and avoid excessive or unnecessary supplementation.

IV. Debunking Misconceptions

Section 4 aims to dispel common misconceptions surrounding the merging of the Paleo and plant-based diets and highlight the areas of common ground between these two approaches.

Contrary to popular belief, the Paleo and plant-based diets are not mutually exclusive. Both emphasize the consumption of whole, unprocessed foods and discourage the intake of refined sugars and processed products. By focusing on these shared principles, individuals can find common ground and create a balanced approach that suits their needs and preferences.

Moreover, it is essential to recognize that individualization and flexibility are key when merging these diets. Each person's nutritional requirements and health goals differ, and the balance between the Paleo and plant-based elements may vary accordingly. It is important to listen to your body, adapt the dietary approach to suit your needs, and regularly monitor your nutritional status to ensure you are meeting your nutrient requirements.

By debunking misconceptions and understanding the shared principles of the Paleo and plant-based diets, individuals can embrace the freedom to create a personalized and balanced approach that optimizes their health and well-being.

In the following section, we will emphasize the significance of seeking professional guidance to ensure a balanced and nourishing dietary approach while merging the Paleo and plant-based diets. The expertise of healthcare professionals and registered dietitians can provide valuable insights and recommendations tailored to individual needs and goals.

V. Seeking Professional Guidance

Section 5 emphasizes the importance of seeking professional guidance when merging the Paleo and plant-based diets. Healthcare professionals and registered dietitians play a critical role in providing evidence-based recommendations, personalized advice, and ongoing support to ensure a balanced and nourishing approach.

5.1 Individualized Approach:

Every individual has unique nutritional needs, health considerations, and personal preferences. Seeking professional guidance allows for a tailored approach that takes into account these individual factors. Healthcare professionals and registered dietitians can assess your specific requirements, such as age, sex, activity level, and any existing health conditions, to provide personalized advice that optimizes your nutrition and overall well-being.

5.2 Nutrient Assessment:

Balancing the Paleo and plant-based diets requires careful consideration of nutrient intake to ensure adequacy. Healthcare professionals and registered dietitians can conduct a thorough nutrient assessment to identify any potential gaps or deficiencies. By evaluating your current dietary patterns, they can offer guidance on specific nutrients of concern, such as protein, iron, calcium, omega-3 fatty acids, and vitamin B12, and provide recommendations for meeting these needs through a balanced approach.

5.3 Meal Planning and Recipe Guidance:

Developing well-balanced meals that merge the Paleo and plant-based elements can be challenging without proper guidance. Healthcare professionals and registered dietitians can offer meal planning assistance and recipe suggestions that align with your preferences and nutritional requirements. They can help you identify appropriate protein sources, recommend specific food combinations to enhance nutrient absorption, and suggest cooking techniques that preserve both nutrition and flavor.

5.4 Monitoring and Adjustment:

The Paleo Green Feast

A balanced approach to nutrition requires regular monitoring and adjustment to ensure ongoing success. Healthcare professionals and registered dietitians can provide guidance on how to monitor your nutritional status, including blood tests and other assessments, to identify any areas that may need further attention. They can also assist with making necessary adjustments to your diet, supplementation, or meal plan based on changes in your health status or evolving nutritional needs.

5.5 Accountability and Support:

Embarking on a dietary journey that merges the Paleo and plant-based diets can be overwhelming at times. Having a healthcare professional or registered dietitian as a trusted resource can provide valuable accountability and support. They can help you navigate challenges, address concerns, and provide ongoing encouragement as you strive to maintain a balanced and nourishing approach to your nutrition.

5.6 Staying Informed:

The field of nutrition is constantly evolving, with new research and insights emerging regularly. Healthcare professionals and registered dietitians stay updated on the latest scientific findings and evidence-based recommendations. By seeking their guidance, you can access accurate and up-to-date information, ensuring that your dietary approach aligns with the most current knowledge and understanding.

In conclusion, seeking professional guidance is essential when merging the Paleo and plant-based diets. Healthcare professionals and registered dietitians bring expertise, personalized advice, and ongoing support to help you create a balanced and nourishing approach that optimizes your health, well-being, and long-term success. By working collaboratively with these professionals, you can navigate the challenges, maximize the benefits, and achieve a harmonious integration of the Paleo and plant-based elements in your diet.

Balancing the Paleo and plant-based diets requires careful consideration of individual needs, preferences, and health goals. It is a journey of self-discovery and self-care, where we learn to create a personalized approach that nourishes our bodies, supports our well-being, and aligns with our values.

Throughout this chapter, we have emphasized the importance of nutrient adequacy and debunked misconceptions surrounding the merging of these two dietary approaches. By recognizing the areas of overlap, such as whole, unprocessed foods, and shared principles, we have empowered ourselves to find common ground and create a well-rounded approach that suits our needs.

Practical tips for meal planning, food combining, cooking techniques, and supplementation have equipped us with the tools to achieve balance and optimize our nutrition. By incorporating a variety of plant-based protein sources, being mindful of iron, calcium, omega-3 fatty acids, and vitamin B12, and seeking guidance when needed, we can ensure our bodies receive the essential nutrients they require.

It is important to remember that balance is not a fixed state, but a continuous journey. We must remain adaptable, listen to our bodies, and make adjustments as necessary. Regular monitoring, evaluation, and consultation with healthcare professionals and registered dietitians will provide valuable insights and support along the way.

As we conclude this chapter, let us approach the merging of the Paleo and plant-based diets with a sense of curiosity, open-mindedness, and self-compassion. Each step we take toward balance and nourishment brings us closer to our health and well-being goals.

The journey of balancing the Paleo and plant-based diets is not just about surviving but about thriving. It is about embracing the diversity of whole, unprocessed foods, nourishing our bodies with vital nutrients, and finding joy in the exploration of culinary possibilities.

So, let us embark on this transformative journey, armed with knowledge, guidance, and the belief that we can achieve optimal nutrition while harmonizing the Paleo and plant-based diets. By prioritizing our health, well-being, and the abundance of nature's offerings, we will thrive on this unique and fulfilling dietary pathway!

Chapter 8

Meal Prep Mastery—Simple and Delicious Recipes for the Modern Caveman

In the fast-paced world we live in, finding time to prepare healthy and nourishing meals can be a challenge. However, with the right strategies and recipes, meal prep will become a powerful tool for maintaining a balanced and nutritious diet. In Chapter 8, we dive into the art of meal prep and provide you with simple and delicious recipes tailored for the modern caveman.

Meal prep is more than just cooking in advance. It is a systematic approach to planning, preparing, and portioning meals ahead of time to streamline your eating habits, and ensure you always have wholesome and satisfying options readily available. By mastering meal prep techniques, you can take control of your nutrition, save time and money, and stay on track with your health goals.

This chapter is designed to inspire and empower you to become a meal prep master. Whether you are following a Paleo, plant-based, or a combination of both diets, these recipes cater to your dietary preferences while offering a variety of flavors, textures, and nutrients.

Throughout this chapter, you will find recipes that prioritize whole, unprocessed ingredients, vibrant fruits and vegetables, lean proteins, beneficial fats, and nutrient-dense carbohydrates. We will guide you through the steps of efficient meal planning, prepping, and storage to optimize freshness, taste, and convenience.

The Paleo Green Feast

Meal prep is not only about practicality, but also about savoring the joy of nourishing meals. We believe that healthy eating should never seem boring or restrictive. With the right recipes and techniques, you can transform your weekly meal prep routine into a creative culinary experience—where you can indulge in flavorful dishes that support your well-being.

By embracing meal prep mastery, you can:

Save Time: By dedicating a few hours each week to meal prep, you can significantly reduce the time spent on cooking and meal decisions throughout the week. This allows you to reclaim precious time for other activities and ensures you always have a satisfying meal ready to go.

Maintain Nutritional Balance: With meal prep, you have control over the ingredients and portions of your meals, ensuring a well-balanced plate every time. You can easily incorporate the recommended amounts of protein, healthy fats, fiber-rich carbohydrates, and an abundance of colorful vegetables to support your overall health.

Improve Portion Control: Portion sizes can be a challenge to manage when eating on the go or dining out. By prepping meals in advance, you can portion them out appropriately, helping you maintain portion control and avoid unwittingly overeating.

Stay Consistent with Healthy Choices: When hunger strikes and time is limited, it's easy to succumb to less nutritious food options. With pre-prepared meals, you have a healthy alternative readily available, ensuring you stay consistent with your dietary choices, even on busy days.

Save Money: By planning your meals in advance, you can make a detailed shopping list, purchase ingredients in bulk, and minimize food waste. This approach helps you save money and make the most of your grocery budget.

In the following sections, we will provide you with an array of delicious and convenient recipes that are specifically designed for meal prep. From hearty breakfast options to flavorful lunches, dinners, and even snacks, these recipes will inspire your taste buds and simplify your journey toward optimal nutrition.

I. Breakfast Bonanza: Energizing Morning Meals

Section 1 focuses on breakfast, the most important meal of the day. These energizing morning meals will jumpstart your day and provide a solid foundation for balanced nutrition. By prepping breakfast in advance, you can ensure a healthy start to your day even when time is limited.

1.1 Overnight Oats and Chia Puddings:

Overnight oats and chia puddings are perfect for busy mornings. By combining rolled oats or chia seeds with your choice of plant-based milk, fruits, and toppings, you can create a delightful and nutritious breakfast option. Prepare several servings in advance, store them in individual containers, and grab one on the go. Customize your creations with different fruits, nuts, and spices to keep things exciting throughout the week.

1.2 Veggie-Packed Egg Muffins:

Egg muffins are a fantastic way to incorporate protein and vegetables into your breakfast. Simply whisk together eggs, your favorite vegetables (such as bell peppers, spinach, onions, and tomatoes), and spices. Pour the mixture into muffin tins and bake until cooked through. These portable and versatile egg muffins can be made in large batches and stored in the refrigerator or freezer for quick reheating in the morning.

1.3 Smoothie Freezer Packs:

Smoothies are a convenient and nutritious breakfast option. To simplify your morning routine, assemble smoothie freezer packs by prepping individual servings of fruits, vegetables, and other smoothie ingredients in freezer bags. In the morning, just grab a pack, add your choice of liquid (such as plant-based milk or water), and blend until smooth. This allows you to enjoy a refreshing and nutrient-packed smoothie in minutes.

1.4 Protein-Packed Pancakes:

The Paleo Green Feast

Pancakes can be made ahead of time and stored in the refrigerator or freezer for quick and easy breakfasts. Go for recipes that include protein-rich ingredients such as almond flour, protein powder, or Greek yogurt. Prepare a batch of pancakes on your meal prep day, let them cool, and store them in individual portions. When ready to enjoy, simply reheat in a toaster or microwave and top with your favorite fruits, nut butter, or yogurt.

1.5 Portable Breakfast Wraps:

Prepare delicious breakfast wraps by filling whole-grain tortillas with scrambled eggs or tofu, sautéed vegetables, and your choice of sauce or condiments. Wrap each breakfast wrap tightly in foil or parchment paper and store them in the refrigerator. In the morning, grab a wrap, heat it up, and savor a protein-packed, grab-and-go breakfast option.

With these breakfast meal prep ideas, you can start your day with a nutritious and satisfying meal—without sacrificing precious time in the morning rush. By preparing these breakfast options in advance, you set yourself up for success, ensuring that your mornings are nourishing, convenient, and delicious. Stay tuned for the next sections where we explore lunch, dinner, and snack options that will further enhance your meal prep mastery!

II. Lunchtime Delights: Satisfying Midday Meals

Section 2 revolves around creating satisfying and nutritious lunches that can be prepared in advance and enjoyed throughout the week. These meal prep ideas ensure that you have a well-balanced and delicious meal to look forward to during your busy workdays.

2.1 Buddha Bowls:

Buddha bowls are a fantastic way to incorporate a variety of flavors, textures, and nutrients into a single meal. Begin by preparing a base of grains such as quinoa, brown rice, or farro. Then, add a mix of colorful vegetables, such as roasted sweet potatoes, sautéed greens, cherry tomatoes, and cucumber slices. Top it off with plant-based proteins like grilled tofu, chickpeas, or marinated tempeh. For extra flavor and creaminess, drizzle your bowl with a homemade dressing or sauce. Prepare the components of the Buddha bowls ahead of time and just assemble them when ready to eat. They can be stored in individual containers and easily transported for a satisfying lunch.

2.2 Mason Jar Salads:

Mason jar salads are a convenient and visually appealing way to pack a variety of vegetables, proteins, and dressings into a portable container. Layer your salad ingredients starting with the dressing at the bottom, followed by sturdier vegetables like cucumbers and carrots, and then leafy greens. Finally, add proteins like grilled chicken, hard-boiled eggs, or roasted chickpeas. Seal the jar tightly and store it in the refrigerator until ready to eat. When it's time for lunch, simply shake the jar to distribute the dressing, and enjoy a fresh and crisp salad.

2.3 Wrap and Roll:

Wraps are versatile and easy to prepare in advance. Choose whole-grain tortillas or collard greens as a wrap base and fill them with your choice of protein, such as grilled chicken, turkey, tofu, or hummus. Add a variety of crunchy vegetables like bell peppers, shredded carrots, and lettuce. Roll up the wraps tightly, secure them with toothpicks or wraps, and store them in the refrigerator. These portable wraps make a satisfying and handheld lunch option that can be enjoyed on the go.

2.4 Grain and Bean Bowls:

Grain and bean bowls offer a hearty and filling lunch option. Start with a base of cooked grains such as quinoa, brown rice, or barley. Then, add a variety of cooked beans like black beans, kidney beans, or chickpeas. Enhance the flavor with sautéed vegetables, herbs, and spices. For an extra burst of freshness, top your bowl with chopped tomatoes, avocado, or a squeeze of lime juice. Prepare the components of the grain and bean bowls in advance and store them in individual containers. When it's time to enjoy your lunch, simply heat them up and savor the satisfying combination of flavors and textures.

2.5 Soup and Stew:

Soups and stews are comforting and nourishing lunch options, especially during colder months. Prepare a large batch of your favorite soup or stew and portion it into individual containers. Popular options include lentil soup, vegetable chili, or hearty minestrone. When ready to enjoy, simply reheat your soup or stew and pair it with a side salad or whole-grain bread for a well-rounded lunch.

By incorporating these lunchtime meal prep ideas into your routine, you ensure that you have a nourishing and satisfying meal to fuel your afternoons. With a little planning and preparation, you can enjoy a variety of flavors, textures, and nutrients without compromising on taste or convenience. Stay tuned for the next sections where we explore dinner and snack options to complete your meal prep mastery!

III. Dinner Delights: Flavorful Evening Meals

Section 3 is dedicated to preparing flavorful and wholesome dinner options through meal prep. These recipes will make your evenings stress-free and ensure that you have a delicious and nutritious meal waiting for you at the end of the day.

3.1 Sheet Pan Meals:

Sheet pan meals are a time-saving and convenient way to prepare a complete dinner with minimal effort. Start by choosing your protein source, such as chicken breast, salmon fillets, or tofu cubes. Combine it with a variety of chopped vegetables like broccoli, bell peppers, zucchini, and cherry tomatoes. Drizzle with olive oil and season with herbs and spices of your choice. Arrange everything on a baking sheet and roast it in the oven. Once cooked, divide the sheet pan meal into individual containers for easy grab-and-go dinners throughout the week.

3.2 Stir-Fries:

Stir-fries are quick, versatile, and perfect for meal prep. Begin by sautéing your choice of protein, such as thinly sliced beef, shrimp, or tempeh, with a medley of colorful vegetables like snap peas, carrots, bell peppers, and mushrooms. Add flavor with a combination of garlic, ginger, soy sauce, or other Asian-inspired sauces. Once cooked, portion the stir-fry into individual containers and pair with cooked rice, quinoa, or cauliflower rice. When it's time for dinner, simply reheat your stir-fry for a delicious and nutritious meal.

3.3 Casseroles and Bakes:

Casseroles and bakes are a comforting and satisfying dinner option that can be easily prepared in advance. Choose recipes that include a balance of protein, vegetables, and whole grains. Lasagnas, enchiladas, and baked quinoa dishes are popular choices. Prepare the casserole or bake in a large dish, portion it into individual servings, and store them in the refrigerator or freezer. When you're ready to enjoy your dinner, simply heat it up and savor the warm and flavorful layers of goodness.

3.4 One-Pot Meals:

One-pot meals are ideal for busy evenings when you want a hassle-free cleanup. Prepare recipes like chili, curry, or vegetable-packed pasta dishes that can be cooked in a single pot or Instant Pot. These meals can often be made in large batches, allowing for easy portioning and storage. Divide them into individual containers, and you'll have a satisfying dinner ready to enjoy with minimal effort.

3.5 Stuffed Vegetables:

Stuffed vegetables offer a creative and nutritious dinner option. Choose vegetables like bell peppers, zucchini, mushrooms, or eggplants as your edible vessel. Prepare a flavorful filling using a combination of grains, legumes, or lean proteins along with herbs, spices, and your favorite seasonings. Stuff the vegetables with the filling, bake them in the oven, and store them in individual containers. Reheat your stuffed vegetables for a delightful and wholesome dinner.

By incorporating these dinner meal prep ideas into your routine, you can enjoy delicious and nourishing meals without the stress of cooking from scratch every night. These recipes provide a balance of flavors, textures, and nutrients, ensuring that your evenings are filled with satisfying and wholesome dinners.

IV. Snack Attack: Nutritious Bites for Anytime Cravings

Section 4 is all about tackling snack cravings with nutritious and flavorful options. These snacks can be prepared in advance and conveniently enjoyed throughout the day, keeping you energized and satisfied.

4.1 Energy Balls and Bars:

Energy balls and bars are perfect for a quick and nourishing snack. Made with a combination of nuts, seeds, dried fruits, and natural sweeteners, these homemade treats offer a balance of protein, healthy fats, and carbohydrates. Prepare a batch of energy balls or bars and store them in the refrigerator or freezer for grab-and-go snacking.

4.2 Veggie Sticks and Dips:

Cut up fresh vegetables like carrot sticks, cucumber slices, and bell pepper strips to create a crunchy and nutritious snack. Pair them with homemade dips like hummus, guacamole, or Greek yogurt-based spreads. Pre-portion the veggie sticks into individual containers and add a dollop of dip for a refreshing and satisfying snack option.

4.3 Roasted Nuts and Seeds:

Roasted nuts and seeds are a satisfying and nutrient-dense snack choice. Choose a variety of nuts and seeds like almonds, walnuts, pumpkin seeds, or sunflower seeds. Toss them with your preferred seasonings and roast them in the oven until golden and fragrant. Portion them into individual containers for convenient snacking throughout the day.

4.4 Yogurt Parfaits:

Create yogurt parfaits by layering Greek yogurt or plant-based yogurt with fresh fruits, granola, and a drizzle of honey or maple syrup. Prepare several parfaits in advance, store them in jars or containers, and enjoy them as a quick and filling snack option.

4.5 Vegetable Chips:

Make your own vegetable chips by thinly slicing vegetables like kale, beetroot, or sweet potatoes. Toss them with olive oil, sprinkle with your favorite seasonings, and bake them in the oven until crispy. Portion them into individual bags or containers for a guilt-free and flavorful snack.

With these snack options, you can tackle cravings and maintain your energy levels throughout the day. By preparing these snacks in advance, you have convenient and nutritious choices readily available whenever hunger strikes.

With Chapter 8's meal prep mastery, you have now unlocked the secrets to simplifying your breakfasts, lunches, dinners, and snacks. These recipes and strategies will transform your approach to meal planning and preparation, allowing you to enjoy a variety of delicious, wholesome, and well-balanced meals throughout the week. Get ready to savor the benefits of meal prep mastery and embark on a culinary journey that promotes optimal nutrition, time-saving convenience, and culinary delight.

V. Satisfying Sweets: Indulgent Treats for a Balanced Palate

Section 5 focuses on satisfying your sweet tooth with indulgent treats that are both delicious and balanced. These recipes will allow you to enjoy desserts without compromising your commitment to a healthy lifestyle.

The Paleo Green Feast

5.1 Fruit-Based Desserts:

Fruit-based desserts offer a naturally sweet and nutritious option. Whether it's a fruit salad, grilled fruit skewers, or baked fruit with a sprinkle of cinnamon, these desserts highlight the natural flavors and sweetness of fresh fruits. Prepare a batch of fruit-based desserts in advance and store them in individual containers for a guilt-free indulgence.

5.2 Chia Pudding Parfaits:

Chia pudding parfaits are a delightful and nutritious dessert option. Create layers of chia pudding made with your choice of plant-based milk, chia seeds, and a touch of sweetness. Alternate the layers with fresh fruits, nuts, and a sprinkle of granola or shredded coconut. These parfaits can be prepared ahead of time and stored in the refrigerator for a creamy and satisfying treat.

5.3 Dark Chocolate Dipped Treats:

Dark chocolate is a delicious and antioxidant-rich treat that can be enjoyed in moderation. Dip fresh strawberries, banana slices, or dried fruits into melted dark chocolate and let them cool until the chocolate hardens. Store these indulgent treats in the refrigerator or freezer for a decadent yet wholesome dessert option.

5.4 Protein-Packed Baked Goods:

Satisfy your cravings for baked goods with protein-packed treats. Use protein powder or incorporate ingredients like almond flour, oats, or Greek yogurt into recipes for cookies, muffins, or energy bars. These baked goods offer a balance of flavors and nutrients, making them a guilt-free option for a sweet treat.

5.5 Nice Cream:

Nice cream is a dairy-free and healthier alternative to traditional ice cream. Blend frozen bananas with a splash of plant-based milk and add your favorite flavors like vanilla extract, cocoa powder, or fresh fruits. Once blended, enjoy the creamy and refreshing nice cream right away or freeze it for later. Serve it in a bowl or as a fun twist, scoop it into a cone for a satisfying dessert experience.

By incorporating these satisfying sweet treats into your meal prep routine, you can enjoy indulgent desserts while maintaining a balanced and wholesome diet. These recipes allow you to satisfy your sweet cravings without compromising your commitment to health and well-being.

With Section 5, you have unlocked the secrets to enjoying desserts guilt-free. Whether it's a fruit-based creation, a protein-packed baked good, or a creamy nice cream, these recipes offer a balance of flavors, textures, and nutrients to satisfy your sweet tooth. Get ready to indulge in these treats as you continue to master the art of meal prep.

By embracing meal prep, you have unlocked the power to take control of your nutrition, save time, and enjoy nourishing meals throughout the week.

Meal prep is not just about convenience; it is a lifestyle that promotes balance, health, and enjoyment in your culinary adventures. Through strategic planning, efficient preparation, and smart storage, you have learned how to simplify your cooking routine, optimize your nutrition, and make the most of your ingredients.

By preparing breakfasts in advance, you ensure that your mornings start on the right foot with energizing meals like overnight oats, egg muffins, or smoothie freezer packs. These ready-to-go options fuel your day and keep you focused and satisfied.

The lunchtime delights, such as Buddha bowls, Mason jar salads, wraps, and grain and bean bowls, have transformed your midday meals into satisfying and nourishing experiences. The convenience of having pre-portioned, balanced lunches readily available has eliminated the need for last-minute decisions or unhealthy takeout options.

Dinner delights, including sheet pan meals, stir-fries, casseroles, and one-pot meals, have made your evenings stress-free and enjoyable. By prepping these flavorful meals in advance, you can unwind after a long day knowing that a wholesome and delicious dinner is waiting for you.

And let's not forget about snack attack! By preparing energy balls, veggie sticks with dips, roasted nuts, yogurt parfaits, and other nutritious snacks, you have conquered those midday cravings and kept your energy levels stable throughout the day.

Finally, the satisfying sweets section has shown you that indulgent treats can still be part of a balanced diet. Whether it's fruit-based desserts, chia pudding parfaits, dark chocolate treats, protein-packed baked goods, or refreshing nice cream, you can enjoy the occasional sweet indulgence, quite guilt-free!

As you conclude this chapter, you have not only learned the art of meal prep, but you have also gained a deeper appreciation for the benefits it brings. Meal prep empowers you to make healthier choices, saves time, reduces food waste, and ensures that your meals align with your dietary goals and preferences.

Embrace the simplicity and convenience of meal prep as you continue on your journey toward optimal nutrition and overall well-being. Experiment with the recipes, customize them to your liking, and enjoy the process of creating nourishing meals that fuel your body and delight your taste buds.

With the mastery of meal prep, you have the tools to conquer the challenges of a busy lifestyle while still prioritizing your health and wellness. So, embark on this culinary adventure, explore new flavors, and savor the delights that meal prep brings to your table. Bon appétit!

Vesla Ekstedt

Chapter 9

Enhancing Physical Performance—Exercise Regimes Complementing the Caveman's Green Table

Here we delve into the realm of physical performance and explore exercise regimes that complement the principles of *The Caveman's Green Table*. Just as our ancestors relied on physical activity to survive and thrive, we too can harness the power of movement to enhance our overall health and well-being.

Exercise is a crucial component of a holistic approach to wellness, working hand in hand with a nutritious diet to optimize our physical performance. By combining the principles of the caveman's diet, which emphasizes whole, unprocessed foods, with tailored exercise regimes, we can unlock our full potential and achieve greater levels of strength, endurance, and vitality.

This chapter will guide you through various exercise regimes, from strength training and cardiovascular workouts to mobility and flexibility exercises. We will explore how these exercises complement *The Caveman's Green Table*, supporting your goals of optimal men's health and overall physical performance.

As we move into this chapter, it's important to remember that exercise is not a one-size-fits-all approach. We each have unique fitness levels, preferences, and goals. Therefore, the exercise regimes presented here are intended to serve as a starting point, offering guidance and inspiration for designing a personalized workout routine that aligns with the principles of *The Caveman's Green Table*.

Here are key ideas about following the right exercise regime for your lifestyle:

I. Strength Training: Building Lean Muscle and Power

Section 1 explores the world of strength training, which forms the foundation of any well-rounded exercise regime. Strength training involves resistance exercises that target your muscles, challenging them to adapt and grow stronger over time. By incorporating strength training into your routine, you can build lean muscle mass, improve your overall strength, and enhance your physical performance.

1.1 Basic Principles of Strength Training:

This section begins by introducing the fundamental principles of strength training. It covers concepts such as progressive overload, which involves gradually increasing the resistance or intensity of your exercises to continually challenge your muscles. You'll also learn about proper form and technique to ensure effective and safe execution of each exercise. Understanding these principles is crucial for maximizing the benefits of your strength training regimen.

1.2 Compound Exercises:
Compound exercises form the core of any strength training program. These are multi-joint exercises that engage multiple muscle groups simultaneously. Examples include squats, deadlifts, bench presses, and pull-ups. Compound exercises help you develop overall strength and stability, improve coordination, and stimulate the release of growth-promoting hormones.

1.3 Targeted Muscle Group Exercises:

In this section, you'll explore exercises that specifically target individual muscle groups, such as the chest, back, arms, shoulders, legs, and core. By focusing on specific muscle groups, you can develop strength and definition in areas that are important for functional movement and aesthetics. This section provides an overview of exercises like bicep curls, tricep dips, lateral raises, and leg presses.

1.4 Equipment and Training Modalities:

Strength training can be performed using various equipment and training modalities. This section introduces different options, including free weights (such as dumbbells and barbells), weight machines, resistance bands, and bodyweight exercises. You'll learn about the benefits and considerations of each modality, enabling you to choose the approach that best suits your preferences and circumstances.

1.5 Periodization and Progression:

Periodization is an essential concept in strength training that involves organizing your workouts into distinct phases to optimize performance and prevent plateaus. This section explains the principles of periodization, including phases of hypertrophy (muscle growth), strength, and power. Additionally, you'll learn about progressive overload and how to progressively increase the difficulty of your workouts to continue making gains in strength and muscle development.

By incorporating strength training into your exercise routine, you not only build lean muscle mass but also enjoy a host of benefits such as increased metabolism, improved bone density, enhanced joint stability, and better overall functional performance. Whether you are a beginner or you are experienced, this section equips you with the knowledge and techniques to embark on a strength training journey that complements the principles of *The Caveman's Green Table*.

II. Cardiovascular Workouts: Building Endurance and Cardiovascular Health

Section 2 focuses on cardiovascular workouts, which play a crucial role in enhancing endurance, cardiovascular health, and overall physical fitness. These exercises elevate your heart rate, increase lung capacity, and improve your body's ability to efficiently deliver oxygen to your muscles. By incorporating cardiovascular workouts into your routine, you can boost your stamina, improve cardiovascular function, and support your goals of optimal men's health.

2.1 Benefits of Cardiovascular Exercise:

This section begins by highlighting the numerous benefits of cardiovascular workouts. Regular aerobic exercise helps improve heart health by strengthening the heart muscle, lowering blood pressure, and reducing the risk of cardiovascular diseases. It also enhances lung capacity, increases energy levels, improves mood, and aids in weight management. Understanding these benefits motivates you to integrate cardiovascular exercise into your fitness routine.

2.2 Types of Cardiovascular Exercises:

There are various types of cardiovascular exercises, each offering unique benefits and catering to different preferences and fitness levels. This section introduces popular options such as running, cycling, swimming, and high-intensity interval training (HIIT). You'll explore the advantages and considerations of each exercise type, allowing you to choose the ones that align with your goals and interests.

2.3 Aerobic vs. Anaerobic Training:

Understanding the difference between aerobic and anaerobic training is crucial when designing your cardiovascular workouts. This section explains the concepts of aerobic and anaerobic exercise, highlighting how each contributes to your overall fitness. Aerobic exercise involves moderate-intensity, sustained activities like jogging, cycling, or swimming. Anaerobic exercise, on the other hand, involves short bursts of high-intensity activities, such as sprinting or HIIT. You'll learn how to incorporate both forms of training into your workouts for optimal results.

2.4 Designing Cardiovascular Workouts:

To effectively integrate cardiovascular exercise into your routine, you need to design structured and progressive workouts. This section provides guidance on designing cardiovascular workouts based on factors such as duration, intensity, frequency, and progression. You'll learn how to set goals, track your progress, and gradually increase the challenge of your workouts to continually improve your endurance and cardiovascular health.

2.5 Cross-Training and Variations:

Cross-training involves incorporating different types of cardiovascular exercises into your routine to promote overall fitness and prevent boredom or overuse injuries. This section explores the benefits of cross-training and provides examples of how you can vary your workouts. By mixing activities like running, swimming, cycling, and HIIT, you can keep your workouts engaging, target different muscle groups, and challenge your cardiovascular system in diverse ways.

By including cardiovascular workouts in your exercise regime, you enhance your body's ability to efficiently utilize oxygen, increase your endurance, and support overall cardiovascular health. Whether you prefer high-intensity intervals, steady-state activities, or a combination of both, this section equips you with the knowledge and techniques to incorporate cardiovascular exercise into your routine while complementing the principles of *The Caveman's Green Table*.

III. Mobility and Flexibility: Enhancing Range of Motion and Joint Health

Section 3 explores the importance of mobility and flexibility exercises, which play a critical role in enhancing range of motion, joint health, and overall movement quality. These exercises improve the flexibility of your muscles and connective tissues, allowing you to move more freely, reduce the risk of injuries, and enhance your overall physical performance. By incorporating mobility and flexibility exercises into your routine, you can optimize your movement patterns and complement the principles of *The Caveman's Green Table*.

3.1 Understanding Mobility and Flexibility:

This section begins by explaining the difference between mobility and flexibility. Mobility refers to the ability of a joint to move freely and efficiently through its full range of motion, while flexibility refers to the length and elasticity of muscles and connective tissues. You'll learn how mobility and flexibility work together to improve overall movement quality and prevent imbalances or restrictions.

3.2 The Benefits of Mobility and Flexibility Exercises:

Engaging in regular mobility and flexibility exercises offers numerous benefits. This section explores how these exercises can help improve posture, enhance athletic performance, prevent injuries, relieve muscle tension and soreness, and promote overall joint health. By maintaining optimal mobility and flexibility, you can move with ease, reduce muscle imbalances, and enjoy a more fluid and efficient movement experience.

3.3 Types of Mobility and Flexibility Exercises:

There are various types of mobility and flexibility exercises that target different areas of the body. This section introduces exercises such as dynamic stretching, static stretching, foam rolling, yoga, and Pilates. Dynamic stretching involves controlled movements that take joints and muscles through a full range of motion. Static stretching involves holding positions to elongate muscles and improve flexibility. Foam rolling is a self-myofascial release technique that targets muscle knots and trigger points. Yoga and Pilates focus on improving flexibility, strength, and body awareness through specific postures and movements.

3.4 Mobility and Flexibility for Specific Muscle Groups:

In this section, you'll explore mobility and flexibility exercises targeting specific muscle groups and areas of the body. These exercises help alleviate tension, improve joint range of motion, and enhance overall movement quality. You'll learn techniques to improve mobility in areas such as the hips, shoulders, spine, ankles, and wrists. By addressing the specific needs of these areas, you can reduce the risk of injuries and enhance your ability to perform functional movements with ease.

3.5 Incorporating Mobility and Flexibility into Your Routine:

To reap the benefits of mobility and flexibility exercises, it's important to incorporate them into your regular exercise routine. This section provides guidance on how to integrate these exercises effectively, including warm-up routines, cool-down stretches, and dedicated mobility sessions. You'll also learn about the ideal frequency, duration, and intensity for mobility and flexibility work, allowing you to tailor your routine to your individual needs and goals.

By incorporating mobility and flexibility exercises into your routine, you can improve your range of motion, optimize movement patterns, and support overall joint health. Whether you're an athlete, fitness enthusiast, or someone looking to move with more freedom and ease, this section equips you with the knowledge and techniques to integrate mobility and flexibility exercises into your routine while complementing the principles of *The Caveman's Green Table*.

IV. Functional Training: Enhancing Everyday Movement and Stability

Section 4 explores the concept of functional training, which focuses on exercises that mimic real-life movements and improve overall functional fitness. Functional training aims to enhance your ability to perform daily activities, sports, and recreational pursuits with efficiency, strength, and stability. By incorporating functional training into your exercise routine, you can improve your movement patterns, reduce the risk of injuries, and optimize your physical performance in everyday life.

4.1 Understanding Functional Training:

This section begins by explaining the principles and benefits of functional training. You'll learn how functional exercises target multiple muscle groups and emphasize coordination, balance, and stability. Unlike traditional gym exercises that isolate specific muscles, functional training aims to improve your ability to perform activities that involve multiple joints and muscle groups, such as lifting objects, squatting, pushing, pulling, and twisting.

4.2 Core Strength and Stabilization:

Core strength is a vital component of functional fitness. This section explores exercises that specifically target the core muscles, including the abdominals, obliques, and lower back. You'll learn how to engage and strengthen your core through exercises like planks, Russian twists, wood chops, and bird dogs. Developing a strong and stable core improves posture, balance, and overall movement control.

4.3 Balance and Proprioception Training:

Balance and proprioception exercises play a crucial role in functional training. This section introduces exercises that challenge your balance and enhance your body's awareness of position and movement in space. Examples include single-leg exercises like lunges and step-ups, as well as exercises that incorporate balance boards, stability balls, or BOSU balls. Improving your balance and proprioception can enhance your stability, coordination, and overall performance in various activities.

4.4 Functional Movements and Compound Exercises:

Functional training emphasizes compound exercises and movements that simulate real-life activities. This section explores exercises such as squats, deadlifts, lunges, pushing, pulling, and rotational movements. These exercises improve overall strength, mobility, and coordination while enhancing your ability to perform daily tasks with ease. By engaging multiple muscle groups and focusing on functional movement patterns, you'll develop the strength and stability needed for a more efficient and injury-resistant body.

4.5 Incorporating Functional Training into Your Routine:

To integrate functional training into your exercise routine, this section provides guidance on structuring your workouts. You'll learn how to incorporate functional exercises alongside other forms of training, such as strength training and cardiovascular workouts. The section also highlights the importance of progression and variety in functional training to continuously challenge your body and stimulate adaptation.

By incorporating functional training exercises into your routine, you enhance your overall movement quality, stability, and functionality in daily life. Whether you're looking to improve your performance in sports, prevent injuries, or simply move with more efficiency and confidence, this section equips you with the knowledge and techniques to integrate functional training into your routine while complementing the principles of *The Caveman's Green Table*.

V. Mind-Body Practices: Balancing Physical and Mental Well-being

The Paleo Green Feast

Section 5 explores the integration of mind-body practices into your exercise regime, promoting the balance of physical and mental well-being. These practices focus on the connection between the mind and body, emphasizing mindfulness, relaxation, and self-awareness. By incorporating mind-body practices, you can enhance your overall sense of well-being, reduce stress, and optimize your physical performance.

5.1 Mindfulness in Exercise:

This section introduces the concept of mindfulness in exercise, which involves bringing conscious awareness to the present moment during physical activity. You'll learn how to cultivate a mindful approach to your workouts, focusing on your breath, sensations, and movements. Mindfulness in exercise enhances your mind-body connection, allowing you to fully engage in the present and experience the joy and benefits of movement.

5.2 Meditation and Breathing Techniques:

Meditation and breathing techniques have long been used to promote relaxation, reduce stress, and improve mental well-being. This section explores various meditation practices, such as seated meditation, walking meditation, or guided visualization, as well as specific breathing exercises that help calm the mind and body. Incorporating these practices into your exercise routine can help you cultivate a sense of inner peace and balance.

5.3 Yoga and Pilates:

Yoga and Pilates are mind-body practices that combine physical movement, breath control, and mindfulness. This section explores the principles and benefits of these practices, including improved strength, flexibility, posture, and body awareness. You'll learn about different yoga styles, such as Hatha, Vinyasa, or Yin, as well as the core principles of Pilates. Integrating yoga and Pilates into your routine enhances your mind-body connection, fosters relaxation, and supports overall physical and mental well-being.

5.4 Active Recovery and Relaxation:

Active recovery and relaxation techniques are essential for restoring and rejuvenating the body after intense workouts. This section explores activities such as gentle stretching, foam rolling, massage therapy, or hydrotherapy that promote muscle recovery, reduce muscle soreness, and support overall relaxation. Incorporating these techniques into your routine helps optimize your body's ability to adapt and progress while promoting a balanced and sustainable approach to training.

By incorporating mind-body practices into your exercise routine, you enhance the connection between your physical and mental well-being. Whether you seek stress reduction, increased self-awareness, or a deeper sense of inner peace, this section equips you with the knowledge and techniques to integrate mind-body practices into your routine while complementing the principles of *The Caveman's Green Table*.

Throughout this chapter, you have delved into the realms of strength training, cardiovascular workouts, mobility and flexibility exercises, functional training, and mind-body practices. Each section has provided valuable insights, techniques, and considerations for incorporating these exercises into your routine.

Strength training has empowered you to build lean muscle mass, increase overall strength, and enhance your physique. By engaging in compound exercises, targeting specific muscle groups, and understanding principles like progressive overload, you have set the foundations for developing more strength and power.

Cardiovascular workouts have improved your endurance, cardiovascular health, and overall stamina. Whether it's running, cycling, swimming, or engaging in high-intensity intervals, you have elevated your heart rate, increased lung capacity, and enjoyed the benefits of improved cardiovascular function.

The exploration of mobility and flexibility exercises has allowed you to enhance your range of motion, joint health, and overall movement quality. By engaging in dynamic stretches, static stretches, foam rolling, yoga, or Pilates, you have improved your flexibility, reduced muscle tension, and promoted overall joint mobility.

Functional training has taken your exercise routine to a new level by focusing on movements that mimic real-life activities. By incorporating core strengthening exercises, balance and stability challenges, and functional movements, you have improved your overall functional fitness and ability to perform everyday tasks with efficiency and strength.

Lastly, the integration of mind-body practices has fostered a deeper connection between your physical and mental well-being. By practicing mindfulness, meditation, breathing techniques, yoga, or Pilates, you have cultivated a sense of balance, reduced stress, and enhanced your overall sense of well-being.

As you conclude this chapter, remember that exercise is not merely a means to an end but a lifelong journey of self-discovery and personal growth. Embrace the exercises that resonate with you, listen to your body's needs, and adapt your routines as you progress. Incorporate a variety of exercise modalities, challenge yourself, and always prioritize proper form and safety.

By complementing the principles of *The Caveman's Green Table* with these exercise regimes, you have created a well-rounded approach to optimizing your physical performance and overall health. Remember, it's not just about the destination but the journey itself—the joy of movement, the satisfaction of progress, and the profound connection between your body, mind, and spirit.

Vesla Ekstedt

Chapter 10

The Impact on Longevity and Disease Prevention—A Scientific Perspective

As we navigate the modern world filled with various health challenges and concerns, understanding the scientific research behind the relationship between diet, lifestyle, and longevity becomes crucial.

Advancements in scientific research have shed light on the powerful influence of nutrition and lifestyle choices on our health outcomes. By examining the latest studies and evidence, we can gain insights into how adopting the principles of *The Caveman's Green Table* can promote longevity, prevent chronic diseases, and enhance overall well-being.

This chapter presents an in-depth exploration of the scientific perspective on the impact of nutrition, physical activity, stress management, sleep, and other lifestyle factors on longevity and disease prevention. By understanding the underlying mechanisms and scientific evidence, we can make informed decisions to optimize our health and make choices that align with the principles of *The Caveman's Green Table*.

Throughout this chapter, we will delve into the following key areas:

I. The Role of Nutrition in Longevity and Disease Prevention

Section 1 explores the pivotal role of nutrition in promoting longevity and preventing chronic diseases. The food we consume serves as the foundation of our health, providing essential nutrients, antioxidants, and bioactive compounds that influence our cellular function, immune system, and overall well-being. By adopting the principles of *The Caveman's Green Table,* we can harness the power of nutrition to optimize our health-span and reduce the risk of age-related diseases.

1.1 Nutrient-Dense Whole Foods:

This section emphasizes the importance of consuming nutrient-dense whole foods as the cornerstone of a longevity-promoting diet. Nutrient-dense foods, such as fruits, vegetables, lean proteins, whole grains, nuts, and seeds, provide a rich array of vitamins, minerals, fiber, and phytochemicals. These nutrients support various physiological functions, reduce inflammation, protect against oxidative stress, and promote overall health.

1.2 Anti-Inflammatory Effects:

Chronic inflammation is a common underlying factor in many age-related diseases. This section explores the link between nutrition and inflammation, highlighting the impact of specific dietary choices on inflammatory markers. Emphasizing an anti-inflammatory diet that includes omega-3 fatty acids, antioxidants, and polyphenols can help mitigate inflammation and reduce the risk of chronic diseases.

1.3 Oxidative Stress and Antioxidants:

Oxidative stress, caused by an imbalance between free radicals and antioxidants in the body, is another factor implicated in aging and disease development. This section discusses how nutrition plays a crucial role in managing oxidative stress. Antioxidant-rich foods, such as berries, leafy greens, and nuts, provide an abundance of phytochemicals that scavenge free radicals, protecting our cells from damage and promoting cellular health.

1.4 Gut Health and Microbiome:

The gut microbiome has emerged as a key player in maintaining overall health and preventing chronic diseases. This section explores the link between nutrition, gut health, and longevity. Consuming a diet rich in fiber, prebiotics, and probiotics supports a diverse and balanced gut microbiome, which in turn influences immune function, nutrient absorption, inflammation, and metabolic health.

1.5 Caloric Restriction and Fasting:

The Paleo Green Feast

Caloric restriction and intermittent fasting have been associated with longevity and health-span extension in various organisms. This section delves into the science behind caloric restriction and fasting, discussing the potential mechanisms that contribute to their beneficial effects. Exploring strategies such as time-restricted eating and periodic fasting can help optimize metabolic health, cellular repair, and longevity.

1.6 Personalized Nutrition:

This section acknowledges the importance of personalized nutrition in optimizing health and longevity. Individual variations in genetics, metabolism, and dietary preferences call for a personalized approach to nutrition. Emerging fields such as nutritional genomics offer insights into how our unique genetic makeup influences nutrient requirements, responses to specific foods, and susceptibility to certain diseases. By embracing personalized nutrition, we can tailor our dietary choices to our individual needs, maximizing the benefits for our long-term health.

Understanding the role of nutrition in promoting longevity and preventing chronic diseases empowers us to make informed dietary choices. By adopting a diet rich in nutrient-dense whole foods, prioritizing anti-inflammatory and antioxidant-rich ingredients, supporting gut health, considering caloric restriction strategies, and personalizing our nutrition, we can optimize our health-span and pave the way for a longer and healthier life. Section 1 sets the stage for exploring the scientific perspective on nutrition's impact on longevity and disease prevention, providing a solid foundation for the chapters ahead.

II. Lifestyle Factors and Their Influence on Longevity and Disease Prevention

Section 2 delves into the impact of lifestyle factors beyond nutrition on longevity and disease prevention. Our lifestyle choices, including physical activity, stress management, sleep, social connections, and other habits, play a significant role in shaping our health outcomes. By understanding the scientific evidence behind these lifestyle factors, we can make informed choices to support our overall well-being and enhance our longevity.

2.1 Physical Activity and Exercise:

Regular physical activity is a cornerstone of a healthy lifestyle and has profound effects on longevity. This section explores the benefits of exercise on cardiovascular health, metabolic function, cognitive function, and overall well-being. We delve into the different types of exercise, including aerobic exercise, strength training, and flexibility training, and their specific contributions to longevity. Moreover, we discuss the importance of finding enjoyable activities and incorporating movement into our daily lives to maintain an active lifestyle.

2.2 Stress Management and Resilience:

Chronic stress has detrimental effects on our health and accelerates the aging process. This section examines the impact of stress on longevity and disease risk, emphasizing the importance of stress management techniques. We explore various practices such as mindfulness meditation, deep breathing exercises, yoga, and other relaxation techniques that promote stress reduction, emotional well-being, and resilience. By cultivating effective stress management strategies, we can enhance our overall health and promote longevity.

2.3 Sleep Quality and Quantity:

Sleep is a vital component of a healthy lifestyle, and its impact on longevity should not be underestimated. In this section, we explore the scientific research linking sleep to various aspects of health, including immune function, cognitive performance, hormone regulation, and cardiovascular health. We discuss the importance of establishing healthy sleep habits, optimizing sleep hygiene, and prioritizing adequate sleep duration to support our overall well-being and promote longevity.

2.4 Social Connections and Community:

The Paleo Green Feast

Human beings are social creatures, and maintaining strong social connections is crucial for our well-being. This section highlights the influence of social connections on longevity and health outcomes. We explore the benefits of having a supportive network, engaging in meaningful relationships, and participating in community activities. We discuss the positive effects of social interactions on mental health, emotional well-being, and physical health, all of which contribute to a longer and more fulfilling life.

2.5 Healthy Habits and Behavior Modification:

Adopting and maintaining healthy habits is essential for long-term health and longevity. This section explores the science behind habit formation and behavior modification. We discuss effective strategies for setting and achieving health goals, breaking unhealthy habits, and building sustainable routines. By understanding the psychology of behavior change, we can overcome obstacles, establish positive habits, and create a lifestyle that supports our long-term health and well-being.

By considering these lifestyle factors and making conscious choices, we can positively influence our longevity and disease risk. Section 2 highlights the importance of regular physical activity, effective stress management, quality sleep, strong social connections, and healthy habits in promoting overall well-being and extending our health-span. Embracing these lifestyle factors in conjunction with the principles of *The Caveman's Green Table* can pave the way for a vibrant, fulfilling, and extended lifespan.

III. Chronic Disease Prevention and Longevity: The Impact of Nutrition and Lifestyle

Section 3 delves into the scientific evidence linking the principles of *The Caveman's Green Table*, nutrition, and lifestyle choices to the prevention of chronic diseases and the promotion of longevity. By understanding the mechanisms through which specific dietary and lifestyle factors influence disease development and progression, we can make informed choices to optimize our health-span and reduce the risk of age-related illnesses.

3.1 Cardiovascular Health:

Cardiovascular disease is a leading cause of mortality worldwide, but its development is often preventable through lifestyle modifications. This section explores the impact of nutrition and lifestyle factors on cardiovascular health. We delve into the effects of a diet rich in fruits, vegetables, whole grains, healthy fats, and lean proteins in reducing the risk of hypertension, high cholesterol, and atherosclerosis. Additionally, we discuss the benefits of regular physical activity, stress management, and smoking cessation in maintaining a healthy cardiovascular system.

3.2 Metabolic Health and Diabetes Prevention:

Metabolic health plays a vital role in preventing chronic conditions such as type 2 diabetes and metabolic syndrome. This section examines the influence of nutrition and lifestyle choices on metabolic health. We explore the effects of a balanced diet, low in refined sugars and unhealthy fats, on maintaining stable blood sugar levels, insulin sensitivity, and healthy body weight. Moreover, we discuss the benefits of regular physical activity, adequate sleep, and stress reduction in preventing metabolic dysregulation and reducing the risk of diabetes.

3.3 Cancer Prevention:

Cancer is a complex and multifaceted disease, influenced by genetic, environmental, and lifestyle factors. This section explores the link between nutrition, lifestyle choices, and cancer prevention. We examine the role of a nutrient-dense diet in providing the necessary antioxidants, phytochemicals, and fiber that help protect against oxidative stress, DNA damage, and inflammation, all of which are implicated in cancer development. Additionally, we discuss the benefits of maintaining a healthy weight, engaging in regular physical activity, and avoiding tobacco and excessive alcohol consumption in reducing cancer risk.

3.4 Neurodegenerative Disorders:

The Paleo Green Feast

Neurodegenerative disorders, such as Alzheimer's and Parkinson's disease, pose significant challenges to aging populations. This section delves into the impact of nutrition and lifestyle choices on brain health and the prevention of neurodegenerative disorders. We explore the benefits of a diet rich in antioxidants, omega-3 fatty acids, and brain-healthy nutrients in supporting cognitive function and reducing the risk of cognitive decline. Additionally, we discuss the importance of mental stimulation, social engagement, and physical activity in promoting brain health and resilience.

3.5 Bone Health:

Maintaining strong and healthy bones is essential for long-term mobility and quality of life. This section examines the role of nutrition and lifestyle choices in promoting bone health and preventing conditions such as osteoporosis. We explore the importance of calcium, vitamin D, and other bone-supporting nutrients in the diet. Additionally, we discuss the benefits of weight-bearing exercises, resistance training, and balance exercises in promoting bone density, strength, and fracture prevention.

By understanding the impact of nutrition and lifestyle choices on chronic disease prevention, we can take proactive steps to optimize our health and promote longevity. Section 3 emphasizes the importance of adopting a nutrient-dense diet, engaging in regular physical activity, managing stress, maintaining a healthy weight, and avoiding harmful behaviors in reducing the risk of chronic diseases. By embracing these principles, we can enhance our health-span and pave the way for a vibrant and disease-free life.

IV. Telomeres and Aging: The Molecular Insights

Section 4 explores the fascinating relationship between telomeres, aging, and the impact of nutrition and lifestyle choices on telomere health. Telomeres are the protective caps at the ends of our chromosomes that play a crucial role in cellular aging and longevity. By understanding the science behind telomeres and their connection to aging, we can explore how nutrition and lifestyle factors can influence telomere length and support healthy cellular aging.

4.1 Telomeres and Cellular Aging:

This section provides an overview of telomeres and their role in cellular aging. Telomeres act as protective caps, preventing the degradation of genetic material and maintaining chromosome stability. Over time, telomeres naturally shorten with each cell division, leading to cellular aging and eventual cell senescence or death. The gradual erosion of telomeres is associated with age-related diseases and shortened lifespan. We delve into the mechanisms underlying telomere shortening and the implications for overall health and longevity.

4.2 Nutrition and Telomere Health:

The impact of nutrition on telomeres is an area of growing interest in scientific research. This section explores the connection between specific dietary components and telomere health. We discuss the effects of antioxidant-rich foods, omega-3 fatty acids, and a balanced diet on supporting telomere length and preventing premature telomere shortening. Additionally, we explore the potential benefits of dietary supplementation with specific nutrients and phytochemicals in preserving telomere integrity.

4.3 Lifestyle Factors and Telomere Health:

Lifestyle factors play a significant role in telomere health and cellular aging. This section delves into the impact of various lifestyle choices on telomere length. We discuss the influence of physical activity, stress management, sleep quality, and tobacco use on telomeres. Regular exercise, effective stress reduction techniques, adequate sleep, and avoiding harmful behaviors can promote telomere maintenance and healthy cellular aging.

4.4 Telomerase and Telomere Maintenance:

Telomerase is an enzyme that can counteract telomere shortening by replenishing telomeric DNA sequences. This section explores the role of telomerase in telomere maintenance and its potential implications for longevity. We discuss the factors that influence telomerase activity and how lifestyle choices, including nutrition and certain behaviors, may impact telomerase expression and function. Understanding telomerase regulation provides insights into potential strategies to support telomere health and potentially extend lifespan.

4.5 Beyond Telomere Length: Telomere Dysfunction and Senescence:

Telomere dysfunction, characterized by critically short or dysfunctional telomeres, can lead to cellular senescence, a state in which cells lose their ability to divide and function properly. This section explores the consequences of telomere dysfunction and cellular senescence on aging and disease. We discuss the role of inflammation, oxidative stress, and other factors in accelerating telomere attrition and cellular aging. Furthermore, we examine lifestyle strategies that may mitigate telomere dysfunction and promote healthy cellular function.

Understanding the intricate relationship between telomeres, aging, and the impact of nutrition and lifestyle choices offers valuable insights into promoting healthy cellular aging and potentially extending health-span. Section 4 highlights the importance of nutrition, stress management, exercise, and other lifestyle factors in supporting telomere health and mitigating telomere shortening. By adopting strategies that preserve telomere integrity, we can optimize our cellular health and promote a longer, healthier life.

V. Longevity-Boosting Strategies: Lessons from Blue Zones and Beyond

Section 5 explores longevity-boosting strategies that have been observed in populations known for their exceptional longevity, such as the Blue Zones. By studying these populations and understanding the commonalities in their lifestyle choices, we can glean valuable insights and practical lessons to apply in our own lives to enhance our longevity and well-being.

5.1 The Blue Zones: Lessons from Long-Lived Populations:

This section delves into the concept of Blue Zones—regions around the world with a high proportion of centenarians (people living 100 years or more). We explore the key characteristics and lifestyle factors that contribute to the longevity of individuals in these regions. From Ikaria, Greece to Okinawa, Japan, we uncover the commonalities among these populations, including their dietary patterns, physical activity levels, strong social connections, and sense of purpose. We discuss the lessons we can learn from these Blue Zones and how we can apply them to our own lives.

5.2 Plant-Based Diets and Longevity:

Plant-based diets have gained recognition for their health benefits and association with longevity. This section examines the scientific evidence supporting the benefits of plant-based diets for longevity. We explore the impact of consuming a predominantly plant-based diet, rich in fruits, vegetables, whole grains, legumes, and nuts, on reducing the risk of chronic diseases and promoting overall health. We also discuss the importance of maintaining a balanced and nutrient-dense plant-based diet to ensure adequate intake of essential nutrients.

5.3 Mindfulness and Longevity:

The practice of mindfulness has gained attention for its potential impact on mental well-being and overall health. This section explores the link between mindfulness and longevity. We discuss the benefits of cultivating mindfulness, including stress reduction, improved emotional well-being, and enhanced resilience. By incorporating mindfulness practices such as meditation, mindful eating, and body awareness into our daily lives, we can positively influence our longevity and overall quality of life.

5.4 Purpose and Meaning in Life:

Having a sense of purpose and meaning in life has been linked to enhanced well-being and longevity. This section explores the importance of finding purpose and meaning in our daily lives. We discuss how aligning our actions with our values, setting meaningful goals, and engaging in activities that bring fulfillment can positively impact our overall health and longevity. We also explore the role of social connections and community involvement in fostering a sense of purpose and belonging.

5.5 Active Aging and Lifelong Learning:

Active aging and ongoing learning play significant roles in promoting longevity and cognitive health. This section emphasizes the importance of staying mentally and physically active as we age. We discuss the benefits of engaging in lifelong learning, pursuing hobbies and interests, and challenging our minds through intellectual stimulation. Additionally, we explore the role of physical activity in maintaining mobility, cognitive function, and overall vitality as we age.

By embracing the lessons from Blue Zones, adopting plant-based diets, cultivating mindfulness, finding purpose in life, and engaging in active aging and lifelong learning, we can enhance our longevity and overall well-being. Section 5 provides practical strategies and insights to guide us on our journey toward a longer, healthier, and more fulfilling life. By incorporating these longevity-boosting strategies into our lives, we can create a blueprint for optimizing our health-span and living our best lives.

By delving into the latest research and scientific evidence, we have gained valuable insights into how our choices can influence our health-span and potentially extend our lifespan.

Throughout this chapter, we have explored the role of nutrition in promoting longevity and preventing chronic diseases. By adopting a diet rich in nutrient-dense whole foods, antioxidants, and anti-inflammatory compounds, we can support our cellular health, reduce the risk of age-related illnesses, and enhance our overall well-being.

We have also delved into the influence of lifestyle factors on our health and longevity. From physical activity and stress management to sleep quality and social connections, our lifestyle choices play a significant role in shaping our health outcomes. By prioritizing these factors and incorporating them into our daily lives, we can optimize our health-span and promote a higher quality of life.

The exploration of telomeres and their connection to aging has shed light on the molecular mechanisms underlying cellular aging. By understanding how telomeres function and the factors that influence their length and integrity, we can make informed choices to support healthy cellular aging and potentially extend our health-span.

Moreover, we have delved into the concept of longevity-boosting strategies, drawing inspiration from Blue Zones and other long-lived populations. By embracing plant-based diets, mindfulness practices, purposeful living, active aging, and lifelong learning, we can tap into the wisdom of these populations and apply it to our own lives, enhancing our well-being and longevity.

As we conclude Chapter 10, it is important to remember that longevity and disease prevention are multifaceted endeavors. It requires a holistic approach that encompasses nutrition, lifestyle choices, mindful living, and ongoing self-care. By adopting the principles of *The Caveman's Green Table,* we have set the foundation for optimizing our health and well-being, aligning with the wisdom of our ancestors and the scientific understanding of our modern world.

Through the integration of nutrition and lifestyle choices, we have the power to shape our health outcomes, prevent chronic diseases, and promote longevity. By embracing the knowledge and insights gained from this chapter, we can embark on a journey of improved health, vitality, and overall well-being.

Let us continue to prioritize our health by nourishing our bodies with wholesome foods, engaging in regular physical activity, managing stress effectively, cultivating mindfulness, nurturing social connections, and pursuing purposeful lives. By doing so, we can pave the way for a vibrant, fulfilling, and extended lifespan, embracing the principles of *The Caveman's Green Table* and the scientific perspective on longevity and disease prevention.

As we move forward, let us carry the lessons learned in this chapter with us, making conscious choices that support our health and well-being. May our efforts to optimize our health-span inspire others and contribute to a world where individuals thrive—not just in survival—but in the pursuit of lifelong vitality and longevity.

Vesla Ekstedt

Chapter 11

The Sustainable Caveman—Adopting a Green Table Lifestyle for Health and the Environment

The principles of *The Caveman's Green Table* not only prioritize our personal well-being but also extend to our responsibilities as stewards of this planet. By adopting a sustainable approach to our dietary choices and lifestyle, we can promote both individual health and the preservation of our environment for future generations.

This chapter explores the intersection of health and sustainability, emphasizing the importance of adopting a Green Table lifestyle. We delve into the impacts of our food choices on the environment, including issues such as greenhouse gas emissions, deforestation, water usage, and biodiversity loss. Additionally, we explore the benefits of sustainable agriculture, plant-based diets, and mindful consumption in mitigating these environmental challenges.

By aligning our dietary and lifestyle choices with sustainable practices, we can create a symbiotic relationship between *our* health and the health *of the planet.* This chapter encourages us to embrace the role of the Sustainable Caveman, acknowledging that our choices have far-reaching consequences—beyond our own well-being.

Throughout this chapter, we will visit the following key areas:

I. The Environmental Impact of Food Choices

Section 1 delves into the profound environmental consequences of our food choices and highlights the urgent need for sustainable practices. By understanding the environmental impact of our dietary decisions, we can make informed choices that prioritize both our health and the health of the planet.

1.1 Carbon Footprint and Greenhouse Gas Emissions:

This subsection explores the significant role of food production in contributing to greenhouse gas emissions, particularly through the production of animal-based foods. We examine the carbon footprint of different dietary patterns, such as the emissions associated with livestock farming, transportation, and deforestation. By embracing a Green Table lifestyle that prioritizes plant-based foods, we can significantly reduce our carbon footprint and mitigate climate change.

1.2 Water Usage and Conservation:

Water scarcity is a pressing global issue, and food production is a major contributor to water usage. In this subsection, we explore the water footprint of different food products and agricultural practices. We discuss the importance of water conservation, such as reducing water-intensive crops and implementing sustainable irrigation techniques. By making conscious choices to consume water-efficient foods and supporting sustainable farming practices, we can contribute to the conservation of this vital resource.

1.3 Deforestation and Biodiversity Loss:

The expansion of agriculture, particularly for livestock feed and the cultivation of crops such as soy and palm oil, has led to extensive deforestation and loss of biodiversity. This subsection delves into the environmental consequences of deforestation, including the destruction of habitats, the loss of species, and the disruption of ecosystems. We discuss the importance of supporting sustainable farming methods that prioritize biodiversity conservation and the preservation of natural habitats.

1.4 Food Waste and its Environmental Impact:

The Paleo Green Feast

Food waste is a significant contributor to environmental degradation. This subsection explores the environmental consequences of food waste, including the emissions generated from decomposing organic waste in landfills. We discuss the importance of reducing food waste through mindful consumption, proper storage, and utilizing food surplus. By minimizing food waste and making use of composting and recycling methods, we can reduce our environmental footprint and promote a more sustainable food system.

1.5 Life Cycle Assessment and Sustainable Food Choices:

Life cycle assessment is a comprehensive approach to evaluating the environmental impact of a product throughout its entire life cycle, from production to disposal. This subsection explores the concept of life cycle assessment as it applies to food production. We discuss the importance of considering the environmental impact of our food choices and opting for sustainable options that have lower resource consumption, reduced emissions, and minimized waste throughout their life cycle.

By understanding the environmental impact of our food choices, we can make conscious decisions that prioritize sustainable practices. Section 1 highlights the interconnectedness of our dietary decisions with carbon emissions, water usage, deforestation, biodiversity loss, and food waste. By embracing a Green Table lifestyle that focuses on plant-based diets, mindful consumption, and supporting sustainable agriculture, we can contribute to a healthier planet and pave the way for a more sustainable future.

II. Sustainable Agriculture and Food Production

Section 2 explores the importance of sustainable agriculture and food production practices in promoting environmental stewardship and long-term food security. By embracing sustainable approaches, we can minimize the environmental impact of food production, support biodiversity, and ensure the availability of nutritious and safe food for future generations.

2.1 Regenerative Farming Practices:

Regenerative farming is an approach that seeks to restore and enhance the health of agricultural ecosystems. This subsection explores regenerative farming practices, such as cover cropping, crop rotation, agroforestry, and the use of organic fertilizers. We discuss how these practices improve soil health, enhance biodiversity, promote water conservation, and reduce the reliance on synthetic chemicals. By supporting regenerative farming methods, we can contribute to the restoration of degraded land and the preservation of ecosystem services.

2.2 Organic Agriculture:

Organic agriculture prioritizes the use of natural inputs and environmentally friendly practices. In this subsection, we delve into the principles and benefits of organic farming, including the avoidance of synthetic pesticides and genetically modified organisms (GMOs). We discuss how organic agriculture promotes soil fertility, biodiversity conservation, and reduces the potential for pesticide residues in food. By choosing organic foods and supporting organic farming practices, we can encourage a more sustainable and ecologically conscious food system.

2.3 Local and Seasonal Food Systems:

The promotion of local and seasonal food systems is a key aspect of sustainable agriculture. This subsection explores the benefits of consuming locally grown and seasonal produce. We discuss how local food systems reduce transportation emissions, support local economies, and promote community resilience. By seeking out locally sourced foods and embracing seasonal eating, we can reduce our carbon footprint and support sustainable food production.

2.4 Biodiversity Conservation:

Biodiversity is vital for the health and resilience of ecosystems. This subsection emphasizes the importance of biodiversity conservation in sustainable agriculture. We discuss the role of diversified cropping systems, the preservation of native plant species, and the promotion of pollinator habitats. By supporting agricultural practices that enhance biodiversity, we can protect crucial ecosystem services, such as pollination, pest control, and soil fertility, which are essential for sustainable food production.

2.5 Sustainable Livestock Farming:

Livestock farming can have significant environmental impacts, but sustainable practices can mitigate these effects. This subsection explores sustainable livestock farming methods, such as rotational grazing, pasture-based systems, and the reduction of antibiotic use. We discuss how these practices can minimize soil degradation, water pollution, and greenhouse gas emissions associated with livestock production. By opting for sustainably raised animal products or reducing our reliance on animal-based foods, we can contribute to more sustainable food systems.

By promoting sustainable agriculture and food production practices, we can transform our food systems to be more ecologically conscious and resilient. Section 2 highlights the importance of regenerative farming, organic agriculture, local and seasonal food systems, biodiversity conservation, and sustainable livestock farming. By supporting these practices and making informed choices as consumers, we can actively participate in creating a food system that nourishes both people and the planet, ensuring a sustainable future for generations to come.

III. The Role of Plant-Based Diets in Sustainability

Section 3 explores the significant role of plant-based diets in promoting sustainability, reducing environmental impact, and addressing the challenges of food production. By shifting towards plant-based dietary choices, we can make a positive contribution to environmental conservation, resource efficiency, and global food security.

3.1 Environmental Benefits of Plant-Based Diets:

This subsection examines the environmental benefits associated with plant-based diets. We discuss how plant-based diets reduce greenhouse gas emissions, land use, and water consumption compared to diets rich in animal products. The production of plant-based foods requires fewer resources and generates fewer environmental pollutants. By adopting a plant-based diet, we can significantly reduce our ecological footprint and contribute to mitigating climate change.

3.2 Reducing Deforestation and Land Conversion:

Deforestation and land conversion for agriculture have devastating consequences for biodiversity and climate change. In this subsection, we explore how plant-based diets help combat deforestation by reducing the demand for land-intensive livestock farming and animal feed production. We discuss the importance of preserving forests and natural habitats, promoting sustainable land use practices, and supporting agroforestry initiatives. By choosing plant-based foods, we can contribute to the preservation of valuable ecosystems and the protection of wildlife.

3.3 Water Conservation and Efficiency:

Water scarcity is a global concern, and the agricultural sector is a significant water consumer. This subsection delves into the water-saving potential of plant-based diets. We discuss how plant-based foods typically require less water to produce compared to animal-based foods. By reducing our consumption of animal products, we can alleviate pressure on freshwater resources and promote water conservation. Supporting sustainable farming practices that prioritize efficient irrigation techniques further enhances water conservation efforts.

3.4 Promoting Sustainable Crop Production:

Plant-based diets encourage the cultivation of diverse crops and promote sustainable farming practices. This subsection explores the benefits of crop diversification, including the promotion of soil health, pest control, and crop resilience. We discuss the importance of supporting farmers who implement sustainable agricultural methods, such as organic farming, permaculture, and regenerative practices. By embracing plant-based diets, we can support sustainable crop production and contribute to the overall health of agricultural ecosystems.

3.5 Food Security and Global Nutrition:

Food security and nutrition are critical issues on a global scale. This subsection highlights how plant-based diets can address these challenges. We discuss how plant-based foods can be more resource-efficient and provide a sustainable solution for feeding a growing global population. By focusing on a diverse range of plant-based foods, we can improve access to nutritious food, reduce malnutrition, and enhance global food security.

By understanding the role of plant-based diets in promoting sustainability, we can make informed choices that align with our health and environmental values. Section 3 emphasizes the environmental benefits of plant-based diets, such as reducing greenhouse gas emissions, conserving water resources, preserving forests, and promoting sustainable agriculture. By embracing plant-based foods, we contribute to a more sustainable food system and foster a healthier planet for future generations.

IV. Mindful Consumption and Waste Reduction

Section 4 explores the importance of mindful consumption and waste reduction in promoting sustainability. By adopting mindful practices and reducing waste, we can minimize our environmental impact and contribute to a more sustainable future.

4.1 Conscious Purchasing Decisions:

This subsection emphasizes the significance of conscious purchasing decisions in sustainable living. We discuss the importance of considering the environmental and social implications of the products we buy, such as choosing products with minimal packaging, opting for sustainably sourced materials, and supporting ethical and fair-trade practices. By being mindful consumers, we can drive demand for sustainable products and encourage businesses to adopt more environmentally friendly practices.

4.2 Reducing Food Waste:

Food waste is a significant environmental issue, and this subsection focuses on strategies to minimize it. We discuss the importance of proper meal planning, smart shopping, and effective storage to prevent food waste at home. We explore creative ways to utilize leftovers, embrace composting to reduce organic waste, and support initiatives that redistribute surplus food to those in need. By reducing food waste, we not only conserve resources, but also address issues of hunger and food insecurity.

4.3 Sustainable Packaging and Recycling:

Packaging waste contributes to environmental pollution and resource depletion. This subsection highlights the importance of sustainable packaging choices and recycling practices. We discuss the benefits of opting for products with minimal packaging, choosing recyclable and biodegradable materials, and supporting companies that prioritize sustainable packaging solutions. We also explore the importance of proper recycling and waste management to minimize the impact of packaging waste on the environment.

4.4 Circular Economy and Product Lifecycles:

The concept of the circular economy is central to sustainable consumption. In this subsection, we delve into the principles of a circular economy, including reducing, reusing, and recycling resources to minimize waste and maximize resource efficiency. We discuss the importance of extending the lifespan of products through repair, repurposing, and sharing, as well as supporting initiatives that promote product and material recycling. By embracing the principles of the circular economy, we can contribute to the transition to a more sustainable and resource-efficient society.

4.5 Conscious Travel and Transportation:

Travel and transportation have environmental implications, and this subsection explores sustainable options. We discuss the benefits of choosing eco-friendly modes of transportation, such as walking, biking, or using public transportation whenever possible. We also explore the concept of conscious travel, which involves making responsible choices to reduce carbon emissions, support local communities, and respect natural and cultural heritage. By adopting conscious travel practices, we can minimize our carbon footprint and contribute to sustainable tourism.

By practicing mindful consumption and waste reduction, we can minimize our environmental impact and promote sustainability. Section 4 emphasizes the importance of conscious purchasing decisions, reducing food waste, sustainable packaging and recycling, embracing the circular economy, and adopting sustainable travel practices. By incorporating these mindful habits into our daily lives, we can play an active role in creating a more sustainable future for ourselves and future generations.

V. Sustainable Living Beyond the Table

Section 5 expands the discussion beyond dietary choices to explore other areas of sustainable living. By adopting sustainable practices in various aspects of our lives, we can further reduce our ecological footprint and contribute to a more sustainable world.

5.1 Energy Consumption and Efficiency:

Energy consumption is a significant contributor to greenhouse gas emissions and environmental degradation. This subsection explores strategies for reducing energy consumption and improving energy efficiency in our homes and daily lives. We discuss the benefits of using renewable energy sources, implementing energy-efficient technologies, practicing energy conservation, and supporting policies that promote renewable energy adoption.

5.2 Waste Management and Recycling:

Waste management is crucial for environmental sustainability. This subsection emphasizes the importance of proper waste segregation, recycling, and responsible waste disposal. We discuss the benefits of recycling common household materials, reducing single-use items, and supporting initiatives that promote waste reduction and recycling programs. By adopting responsible waste management practices, we can minimize the amount of waste sent to landfills and conserve resources.

5.3 Water Conservation:

Water is a precious resource, and this subsection explores strategies for conserving water in our daily lives. We discuss the importance of water-efficient fixtures, responsible water usage, and reducing water waste. We explore practices such as collecting rainwater, using water-saving appliances, and practicing mindful water use in our homes and gardens. By adopting water conservation habits, we can contribute to the preservation of freshwater resources and promote sustainable water management.

5.4 Reconnecting with Nature:

Reconnecting with nature is essential for our well-being and environmental consciousness. This subsection emphasizes the benefits of spending time in nature, developing a sense of awe and appreciation for the natural world, and engaging in activities that foster environmental stewardship. We discuss the importance of supporting conservation efforts, participating in outdoor recreation responsibly, and cultivating a deeper connection with the natural environment.

5.5 Community Engagement and Advocacy:

Community engagement and advocacy play a vital role in promoting sustainability. This subsection explores ways to get involved in local sustainability initiatives, such as community gardens, environmental organizations, and advocacy groups. We discuss the importance of raising awareness, advocating for sustainable policies, and supporting local businesses that prioritize environmental responsibility. By actively engaging with our communities and advocating for sustainable practices, we can drive positive change on a larger scale.

By embracing sustainable living beyond the table, we can make a holistic and meaningful contribution to environmental sustainability. Section 5 highlights the significance of energy consumption and efficiency, waste management and recycling, water conservation, reconnecting with nature, and community engagement and advocacy. By adopting these sustainable practices, we can collectively work towards a more sustainable future and create a positive impact on our planet.

By exploring the interconnectedness of our dietary choices, mindful consumption, waste reduction, sustainable agriculture, and sustainable living practices, we have gained valuable insights into the transformative power of our actions.

Throughout this chapter, we have learned how our food choices impact the environment, from carbon emissions and water usage to deforestation and biodiversity loss. We have recognized the urgent need to shift towards sustainable agriculture practices that prioritize regenerative farming, organic methods, and the preservation of local and seasonal food systems. By embracing plant-based diets, we can significantly reduce our carbon footprint, conserve water resources, and contribute to the preservation of natural habitats.

Moreover, we have delved into the importance of mindful consumption and waste reduction. By making conscious purchasing decisions, reducing food waste, embracing sustainable packaging, and supporting the principles of the circular economy, we can minimize our environmental impact and promote a more sustainable future. Our actions as consumers can drive change and encourage businesses to adopt more eco-friendly practices.

We have also explored the broader aspects of sustainable living, including energy consumption and efficiency, responsible waste management, water conservation, reconnecting with nature, and community engagement. By incorporating these practices into our daily lives, we can further reduce our ecological footprint and promote a holistic approach to sustainability.

As we conclude Chapter 11, it is important to remember that the choices we make today have a profound impact on the future of our planet. By embracing a Green Table lifestyle, we have the opportunity to create a positive ripple effect that extends beyond our own health and well-being. We can contribute to the preservation of natural resources, the protection of biodiversity, and the mitigation of climate change.

Let us carry the knowledge gained from this chapter with us, and let it inspire us to take action. By adopting sustainable practices in our daily lives, we can be agents of change, paving the way for a more sustainable and resilient future. Our collective efforts can contribute to a world where the principles of *The Caveman's Green Table* are not only embraced for personal health but also for the preservation of our environment.

Vesla Ekstedt

Closing Remarks

In *The Caveman's Green Table: Paleo and Plant-Based Lifestyle for Men's Health*, we have embarked on a journey that explores the intersection of ancestral wisdom, modern science, and sustainable living. This book has provided a comprehensive guide to adopting a healthy and environmentally conscious lifestyle that prioritizes men's health, wellness, and the well-being of our planet.

Throughout the chapters, we have explored the principles of *The Caveman's Green Table,* which encompasses the best of both worlds: the nutrient-dense, whole foods approach of the Paleo diet and the sustainable, plant-based philosophy. By merging these two dietary frameworks, we have discovered a powerful and balanced approach to nourishing our bodies and protecting the environment.

The Genesis of Diet: A Historical Perspective on Cavemen and Green Table set the foundation by exploring the ancestral roots of human nutrition and the importance of incorporating plant-based foods in our diets. We learned from our ancient predecessors and gained insights into the natural synergy between humans and the earth's bountiful offerings.

In The Paleo Blueprint: Understanding the Caveman's Diet and Lifestyle, we delved into the principles of the Paleo diet and lifestyle, examining the benefits of consuming nutrient-dense, unprocessed foods and engaging in physical activities that mimic our ancestors. We learned how to embrace our evolutionary heritage while adapting it to our modern lives.

Unraveling the Green Table: Exploring the Fundamentals of Plant-Based Nutrition enlightened us about the power of plant-based eating. We discovered the abundance of essential nutrients and antioxidants found in plant foods, and how they can support men's health, boost vitality, and contribute to disease prevention.

The Perfect Blend: Merging Paleo and Plant-Based Diets for Optimal Men's Health showed us that the combination of Paleo and plant-based principles can create a harmonious approach to nutrition. We learned how to strike the right balance between animal-based and plant-based foods, optimizing our nutrient intake and promoting sustainable food choices.

Protein Paradox: Addressing the Common Myths and Realities of Protein Sources dispelled misconceptions surrounding protein intake, highlighting the abundance of plant-based protein sources and their ability to support muscle growth, recovery, and overall health. We gained a deeper understanding of the protein needs of men and discovered the diverse options available to meet those needs—without relying solely on animal products.

Power Foods: Embracing the Bounty of Nature for Energy and Vitality introduced us to a vibrant array of nutrient-dense foods. We explored the benefits of incorporating superfoods, adaptogens, and functional ingredients into our diets, fueling our bodies with optimal nutrition and supporting our overall well-being.

Ensuring Adequate Nutrition While Balancing Paleo and Plant-Based Diets showed us how to thrive on a well-rounded and balanced diet. We learned about essential nutrients, supplementation strategies, and meal planning techniques that help us meet our nutritional needs while adhering to the principles of *The Caveman's Green Table*.

Meal Prep Mastery: Simple and Delicious Recipes for the Modern Caveman empowered us with practical tools and techniques for meal preparation. We discovered how to streamline our cooking process, maximize convenience, and make healthy eating an enjoyable and sustainable part of our lifestyle.

Enhancing Physical Performance: Exercise Regimes Complementing the Caveman's Green Table emphasized the importance of physical activity and tailored exercise regimens to support men's health. We learned how to optimize our workouts, enhance performance, and maintain an active lifestyle that aligns with the principles of *The Caveman's Green Table*.

The Paleo Green Feast

The Impact on Longevity and Disease Prevention: A Scientific Perspective shed light on the intricate connection between our dietary choices, lifestyle factors, and their impact on longevity and disease prevention. We explored the scientific evidence behind *The Caveman's Green Table* principles, understanding how they contribute to optimal health and well-being throughout the lifespan.

Finally, The Sustainable Caveman: Adopting a Green Table Lifestyle for Health and the Environment concluded our journey by highlighting the critical role of sustainability. We explored the environmental impact of our food choices, the importance of mindful consumption, waste reduction, and adopting sustainable practices in various aspects of our lives. We recognized our responsibility as stewards of the Earth and the power we hold to make a positive impact on our planet through our choices.

In closing, *The Caveman's Green Table: Paleo and Plant-Based Lifestyle for Men's Health* has provided a comprehensive roadmap for men seeking to optimize their health, embrace sustainable practices, and align their well-being with the preservation of our planet. By adopting the principles outlined in this book, we can nourish our bodies, fuel our performance, and contribute to a healthier and more sustainable world.

Let us embrace the wisdom of our ancestors, the advancements of modern science, and the power of our choices to live a life of vitality, longevity, and environmental consciousness. Together, we can make a difference and create a legacy of health and sustainability for generations to come.

www.ingramcontent.com/pod-product-compliance
Lightning Source LLC
Chambersburg PA
CBHW071156130726
47998CB00002B/524